The Activist's Guide to t]

The Activist's Guide
to the Internet

Fiona Osler & Paul Hollis

Prentice
Hall

An imprint of **Pearson Education**

London · New York · Toronto
Sydney · Tokyo · Singapore · Madrid
Mexico City · Munich · Paris

PEARSON EDUCATION LIMITED

Head Office:
Edinburgh Gate
Harlow CM20 2JE
Tel: +44 (0)1279 623623
Fax: +44 (0)1279 431059

London Office:
128 Long Acre
London WC2E 9AN
Tel: +44 (0)20 7447 2000
Fax: +44 (0)20 7240 5771

First published in Great Britain in 2001

© Pearson Education Limited 2001

ISBN 0-13-087922-3

Many of the designations used by manufacturers and sellers to distinguish their products are claimed as trademarks. Pearson Education Limited has made every attempt to supply trademark information about manufacturers and their products mentioned in this book. A list of trademark designations and their owners appears on page xii.

While the publisher and authors have made every effort to ensure that all entries were correct when this book went to press, the internet changes so rapidly that there may now be website addresses that have moved or ceased to become operational. The publisher and authors can accept no responsibility for any loss or inconvenience sustained by the reader as a result of the content of this book.

British Library Cataloguing-in-Publication Data
A catalogue record for this book is available from the British Library.

10 9 8 7 6 5 4 3 2 1

Typeset by Pantek Arts Ltd.
Printed and bound by Biddles of Guildford and King's Lynn.

The publishers' policy is to use paper manufactured from sustainable forests.

Contents

6	The Developing World and the Internet 78

7	Hacking, Censorship and Liberty Online 88

8	Women Online 105

9	Alternative Media 114

Foreword

The political challenge of the twenty-first century is how democracy, the rule of the people, can succeed against plutocracy, the rule of the corporations. Ironically, the very technology that has extended the global reach of the transnational corporations, is providing the people with a means of subverting their power.

The new technology enables the corporations to combine maximum centralized control with maximum local flexibility. But it also enables the millions of people whose quality of life is threatened by this new domination, to develop their own means of co-ordination and counter control.

Just as the invention of the printing press enabled dissent to flourish and qualitatively strengthened popular pressure for the right to vote – the foundations of democracy – so the internet has given an electrical current to all the grass roots movements and networks, which, from the late Sixties onwards, have been inventing new more powerful, participatory forms of democracy. This book is an indispensable handbook for everyone who is responding ingeniously to the threat of corporate takeover and using the net to make democracy qualitatively more subversive.

What is it about the chemistry between this turn of the century participatory democracy and the internet, that enables them together to generate new sources of power? A common feature of the radical movements of the last twenty years is their challenge to established knowledge and the authorities who hold this knowledge close to their chests. Students demanded to participate in the running of the universities, challenging their teachers' claim to omniscience; feminists overturned the presumption that male professionals knew what was best for them; shop-floor workers rebelled against management prerogatives whether in the public or the private sector; and the green movement arose from a profound scepticism about science and the values driving both its development and its application.

In different ways these movements all assert, in both their theory and their practice, the importance of the knowledge and insights of people who are subordinate, oppressed, marginal, local – in fact the majority of the world's population. They value practical knowledge, knowledge that comes from experience.

But they do not stop at the individual experience or the parochial horizon. A distinctive feature of all these radical movements, now reaching a climax with the anti-capitalist movement that has been mobilizing so dramatically against the World Trade Organization is the extraordinary reach of their networks. These informal networks, from the internationally replicated 'consciousness-raising' groups of the women's movement to the affinity groups of the direct action movement, have many purposes but crucial is their role in sharing a variety of kinds of knowledge, or clues to knowledge: practical and theoretical, intuitive and statistical, historical and speculative. This horizontal method of building up a common memory, a shared perspective, even agreed tactics is new. In the past most radical political organizations have, like those of the establishment, concentrated knowledge at the top. I don't want to romanticize: the moments of structurelessness that social movements experience can produce their own forms of tyranny, as has been frequently analyzed. The importance of the net is that it provides a technology almost tailor-made to give constant momentum to this sideways speading of knowledge. The timely production of *The Activist's Guide to the Internet* will help to make sure we realize that potential.

We should celebrate this breaking of the experts' monopoly of knowledge and the sideways spread of a great diversity of knowledge not for its own sake but because of what it means for the strengthening of democracy. Representative democracy is good – and necessary – for enabling everyone to participate, periodically, in society-wide decisions about the way they would like to be governed. But it is too formal, too much on the outside of society, too vulnerable to take over by the powerful and the unaccountable to enable the people genuinely to participate in the decisions that shape their lives. The internet provides us with the means to develop new realistic mechanisms of knowledgeable participation. We are only in the early experimental stages of inventing those mechanisms. If you are not already an inventor of the new democracy this book will make you one.

Hilary Wainwright
Editor
Red Pepper

Preface

The Internet is the censor's biggest challenge and the tyrant's worst nightmare... Unbeknown to their governments, people in China, Iraq and Iran, among other countries, are freely communicating with people all over the world.

ROLLING STONE

In his 1996 book, *Navigating in Cyberspace* (published by General Distribution Services), Frank Ogden, a leading Canadian futurist, warns 'the next decade will make the past look tame ... within 10 years, the technology that is hardly out of the starting gate will change 90 percent of our culture and society'.

Since the digital revolution of the 1970s, computer-mediated technology has dramatically changed the way we communicate. Just as the printing press, telegraph and the telephone were responsible for communication leaps, so is the internet today. As mainstream media become more subject to censorship and stifled by the need to make money at all costs, sources of information that are non-partisan are increasingly difficult to find. The web lets people communicate with relative impunity and to a large extent in the most democratic of ways.

This guide looks at how those involved in left politics, civil society and progressive movements and causes can make best use of the net. There are a myriad of activist groups, non-governmental organizations, political parties and associations on the net, and the systems they employ, for the most part, are working well. 'Multi-organizational networks' are allowing activists from all parts of the world to keep in touch, share strategies and information and co-ordinate mass activities on a global scale.

The Web and e-communications have revolutionised environmental and social justice campaigning and, arguably, helped to nurture a new north–south dialogue about democracy, social justice, development and human rights in an increasingly globalised world.

JOHN VIDAL, *THE GUARDIAN* 13 JANUARY 1999

As the net has become larger and more complex, it has expanded to encompass an incredible diversity of people, purposes and activities. Aerospace companies engaged in weapons manufacture now share the web with anti-war organizations; governments with dissident groups; multinational corporations with anti-capitalist activists; home shopping companies with anti-consumerist campaigns …

The potential for participatory democracy and bottom-up politics, campaigning, direct action, information exchange, education, outreaching and a hundred other activities covering politics, poverty, land rights, justice, exploitation, environmental preservation, indigenous peoples, guerrilla struggles and women's rights grows daily.

The net, for the first time in history, provides an opportunity for small-scale, grass-roots organizations with limited resources to compete for attention on virtually equal terms with governments and multinationals with millions to spend. No activist group or individual can afford to ignore it.

This guide provides an insight into some of the things already achieved by activists on the internet, and shows how *you* can use the net to help achieve your own activist objectives. The accompanying CD-ROM provides everything you need to carry out e-mail campaigns, create your own website and link up with like-minded individuals and organizations around the world … in short, to dramatically improve your impact and effectiveness. Best of all, you can achieve this without being a computer whizz and within a matter of days!

Please load the accompanying CD for clickable links to websites mentioned in the book.

Part One

Spiders in the Web: Online Activism

1 Reclaiming Technology

A voice from the jungle

A possibly apocryphal story tells us that, using a laptop plugged into the lighter socket of an old pickup, sub-commandante Marcos (www.elzn.org) has become a familiar figure in cyberspace. Faster than they can be published in Mexican newspapers, from La Garrucha and Guadalupe Teypeyac, communiqués flow across the electronic ether reaching countries as distant as Great Britain, Italy, Germany and Russia.

In the hopes of establishing an autonomous state, the largely poor indigenous people of Chiapas, Mexico have long been fighting a political battle with the Mexican authorities. The Zapatista movement is demanding democracy, civil rights, land and jobs for the people of Chiapas. When the Mexican army came into Chiapas to suppress protests by arresting community leaders and burning villages, the Zapatistas took up arms and began a guerrilla war and the internet has been a central part of their strategy.

On New Year's Day 1984, sub-commandante Marcos announced via the internet the take-over of San Cristobal. Since then, the Zapatista movement has moved away from using the mainstream press to publicize their cause. To date, apart from a few journals, newspaper and magazine articles in the more liberal press the Zapatista struggle has been subject to heavy censorship. By extending their political reach through the internet, the Zapatistas have gone global and what ten years ago would have remained a relatively local issue with little international support has captured the attention of the world.

Try typing 'Zapatista' into any search engine and you will find dozens of newsgroups, websites and archives about Marcos, Chiapas and the solidarity movements supporting the Zapatista struggle. Information on atrocities in Chiapas – which include torture, rape and summary executions – and the use of the militia has been placed on websites, bulletin boards and in newsgroups. In turn, this information has been the basis for flyers, pamphlets, books and even a film, all of which have helped to spread the Zapatista cause in many different ways.

Mass demonstrations in the USA, fax and e-mail campaigns in Europe, pickets of Mexican embassies across the globe ... these events have often been organized by e-mail and publicized on websites. Reports have then been uploaded back onto the net to continue the spread of information. The capacity the net offers in terms of interaction means information no longer flows in one direction only. Unlike the mainstream media, the internet allows many-to-many communication and, more importantly, a means of taking action either physically or from the comfort of your armchair.

The result has been, not only to inspire the Zapatista movement, but also to force the Mexican government, aware that the eyes of the world are now watching them, to think twice before committing a new outrage.

> Try typing 'Zapatista' into any search engine and you will find dozens of newsgroups, websites and archives.

Just as mountain men, gauchos and poor farmers have sought independence through the flight to and colonisation of new lands, so cyberspace pioneers have carved out new spaces and filled them with their own activity.

HARRY CLEAVER IN *THE ZAPATISTAS AND THE ELECTRONIC FABRIC OF STRUGGLE*

(www.ecoutexas.edu/homepages/faculty/cleaver/chiapas.html)

Internet use by the Zapatista movement is even more remarkable when put into the context of the standard forms of communication within Mexico. Here, telegrams are still relied on and communal televisions and radios are often the only way for people to keep up to date on affairs in and outside the country. Access to the internet belongs to only a small elite. The movement has got round this with its use of solidarity and support groups throughout the world. By circumventing the state through the net in conjunction with the conventional tools of political activism such as sit-ins, demonstrations, vigils and occupations, the Zapatista movement has provided a new framework for those fighting for democracy and human rights.

Very soon after the struggle took to the internet in the late 1980s the Zapatistas recognized how valuable the net could be for gaining international support. As sub-commandante Marcos wrote at the time,

> *We learned that there were marches and songs and movies and other things that were not war in Chiapas, which is the part of Mexico where we live and die. And we learned … that 'No to war!' was said in Spain and in France and in Italy and in Germany and in Russia and in England and in Japan and in Korea and in Canada and in the United States and in Argentina and in Uruguay and in Chile and in Venezuela and in Brazil … And so we saw that there are good people in many parts of the world.*

These 'good people' included Usenet newsgroups, activists on PeaceNet, environmental activists, feminists, students, lecturers, labour movement officials, humanitarian groups and other indigenous peoples' networks. Messages received in newsgroups and through e-mail are re-posted and translated and spread to other individuals and groups, all the while building stronger and better informed networks of resistance. These networks have brought impartial and non-governmental observers and journalists to the region. Witnessing for themselves the difficulties faced by the people of Chiapas, observers, for example the human rights group Peace Brigades International (PBI) (www.igc.apc.org/pbi/index.html), have acted directly. This international non-governmental organization (NGO) supports those struggling for human rights with non-violent intervention, by acting as 'unarmed bodyguards' for human rights defenders under threat. The volunteers working in Chiapas not only accompany human rights defenders but monitor the activities of para-military and governmental forces, using the internet to post their own accounts. If an atrocity takes place or a human rights defender is threatened, they send out an action alert, by telephone, fax and e-mail. E-mails are sent to PBI supporters and members across the world, giving information on the attack or potential attack and asking for people to send e-mails to the Mexican government and foreign embassies to ask for support and in protest. This has proved to be a remarkably effective technique, and PBI believes it has saved lives, not only in Chiapas but in the other parts of the world in which they work, including Colombia and the Balkans.

In case after case, human rights groups monitoring from the sidelines of conflict have added their commentary via the internet. All this is possible at the touch of a mouse. Altogether it

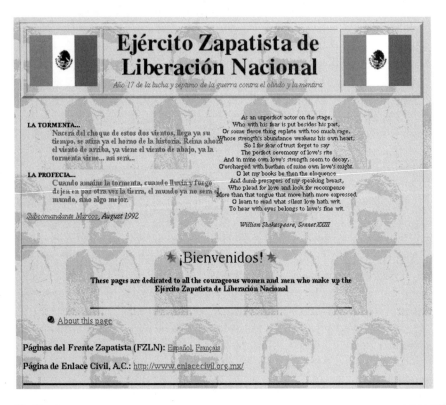

Ya Basta

means that people who have used the net to find out more about the Zapatista movement have been better informed and far more able to make a personal assessment of the situation than those informed by the mainstream media.

Peace Brigades International

"Without the accompaniment of Peace Brigades, I would not be alive today."
Amilcar Mendez, CERJ, Guatemala

making space for peace

I Castellano I Deutsch I Français I Italiano I Nederlands I Svenska I   Last updated 20 June 2000

Peace Brigades International (PBI) is a grassroots organization that explores and promotes nonviolent peacekeeping and support for human rights.

When invited, we send teams of volunteers into areas of political repression and conflict. The volunteers accompany human rights defenders, their organizations, and others threatened by political violence. Those responsible for human rights abuses usually do not want the world to witness their actions. The presence of volunteers backed by an emergency response network thus helps deter violence. In this way, we create space for local activists to work for social justice and human rights.

Where does PBI work?
Currently, Peace Brigades International has long-term projects in Colombia, Indonesia/East Timor, and Haiti, as well as joint projects with other organizations in the Balkans and Chiapas, Mexico and a new project in Mexico.

How can I help?
PBI volunteers and supporters around the world demonstrate that individuals working together can act boldly as peacekeepers even when governments cannot or will not. You can help in a variety of ways. The effectiveness of our volunteers depends directly on the support that we can draw on. More...

What's New
Building Peace in the Aftermath of War
in Kosovo/a and new initiatives in the Balkan Peace Team
What they say about us
What people we have worked with think of PBI
A day in PBI Colombia
New page takes you through a typical day on the project
PBI volunteers in West Timor Camps
Local humanitarian organizations threatened

What You Can Do
Become a member/supporter
Join the Emergency Response Network (ERN)
Volunteer on a PBI project
Participate in a delegation
Help with outreach and public relations

About the Projects
Colombia I Indonesia/East Timor I Haiti I Mexico
Joint projects with others: Chiapas I the Balkans
Archives of closed projects:
Guatemala I N. America I Sri Lanka I

About Peace Brigades International
What we do
Awards for PBI
Read the book about PBI's work
History and structure
Our mission statement
Annual reports, financial information and donors

Country Groups

Australia	France	Spain
Aotearoa/NZ	Germany	Sweden
Belgium	Italy	Switzerland
Britain	Netherlands	United States
Canada	Norway	

Publications
PBI Project Bulletin Archive
Emergency Response Network Alerts
Reports from: the Balkans I Colombia I Haiti
Archived reports from: Guatemala I N. America
Bibliography
Directory of organizations in: Colombia I Guatemala
Links to related organizations

Search this site   powered by FreeFind
[ ] **Find!**

Translate this page automatically

Mario Calixto, a human rights defender from Colombia, with a PBI volunteer the day after an attempt on his life was prevented by PBI volunteers. Photo: PBI

International Office
5 Caledonian Road
London N1 9DX U.K.
Tel: 44-020-7713-0392
Fax: 44-020-7837-2290
Email: pbiio@gn.apc.org

This is the official home page of Peace Brigades International.

Questions or comments about the site?
Contact Jonathan Woodbridge, the PBI Web Coordinator, at pbiweb@mycmail.com

Peace Brigades International

The birth of the internet

It is one of life's great ironies that what is today an open and largely uncontrolled medium, and perhaps the single greatest tool for democracy and individual empowerment, began life as a top-secret military network designed for the purpose of waging nuclear war.

There are many conflicting histories of the internet, perhaps unsurprisingly given the chaotic nature of the net itself. But the basics are clear. In the 1960s, the US Department of Defense (DoD) began to worry about the fact that its highly sophisticated nuclear missile capabilities were vulnerable to an attack on its lines of communication. A Soviet missile attack on its main command centre, or on the communications lines needed to carry launch commands to the individual missile bases scattered around the country, could render it unable to operate. The problem was thrown at the Pentagon's Advanced Research Projects Agency (ARPA).

ARPA decided that the answer was a national communications network in which there were hundreds or thousands of different routes a message could take. If one route was damaged or destroyed, the message would simply find another route to its destination. The result was the creation, in 1969, of ARPANET (although its existence wasn't made public until 1972).

ARPANET proved itself such a useful means of communication that private companies and research institutes involved in defence work became involved, as did universities where defence research was undertaken. The universities were quick to see the potential of a communications network of this kind, and the US government came under pressure for academics of all disciplines to have access to it. When the DoD replaced ARPANET with a new military communications network, what had been ARPANET was effectively handed over to US universities. They joined forces with the UK Joint Academic NETwork (JANET) to form the beginnings of a worldwide academic network.

The internet was still a closed network, restricted to academics, but students were gradually permitted access. Some graduating students, who had become so enamoured of the net that they didn't want to lose access when they left college, made informal arrangements for dial-in access after leaving. Demand soon became so great that private companies were formed to offer internet access to individuals. The internet as we know it today was born.

Digital democracy

Mainstream politics has been quick to see the value of the net. In North America, the 1996 presidential campaign was seen as a landmark in politics on the net, with all the major candidates having websites. Today, candidates for office are conducting debates over the net and using websites to recruit campaign workers and in some cases to spread dis-information about their political opponents. Recently Congress voted to match online donations with funding as they have done in the past for more old-fashioned means of raising money.

In the UK, the Labour government has promised e-government services by 2008 and has begun to solicit comments from the public for its policy. The net has played a key role in Desert Storm, the conflict in the former Yugoslavia, in the Tiananmen Square massacre and, increasingly, in international security.

In 1995 a paper produced for the Pentagon emphasized that by monitoring public message traffic and alternative news sources on the net, early warnings of possible conflict could be picked up. According to the Pentagon, where the net is virtually the only means of communication, internet messages within regions under authoritarian control can be useful sources of intelligence. Much talk is made of using the internet in counter-intelligence and, offensively, as a medium in psychological warfare, described as helping to achieve 'unconventional warfare objectives'.

While governments around the world are struggling to devise legislation to cope with the internet, currently it is still a place which largely defies government rule. Internet commentators all tend to highlight the lack of control and structure to the net, and political observers point to it as the closest example we have to pure anarchy.

There is a strong libertarian bent to the net. Early users tended to be anti-government, anti-hierarchy, anti-big business and anti-censorship, and this culture is still very strong today. The Electronic Frontier Foundation (EFF) (**www.eff.org**), per-

> The internet as we know it today was born.

haps, best characterizes this phenomenon. EFF is the main advocacy and campaigning force against censorship and protection of privacy on the net. EFF believes democracy is a central facet of the net, and that the internet is a tool for the empowerment of people against centralized and non-democratic control.

The net is having a tangible effect on the social, cultural, economic and political lives of millions. What we are beginning to witness today, and will become ever more visible in the coming years, is a battle over the use and ownership of information. While most politicians and corporate leaders believe that the future of capitalism lies in the commodification of information, activists see the easy international dissemination of information as their most powerful tool yet. A recent Rand study ('Cyber War is Coming!' by Jonn J. Arquilla and David Ronfeldt, *Comparative Strategy*, vol. 12, 1993, www.rand.org) concluded that 'the information revolution … disrupts and erodes the hierarchies around which institutions are normally designed. It diffuses and redistributes power, often to the benefit of what may be considered weaker, smaller actors'.

Rather than merely 'fitting in' to pre-existing social processes, the internet can, if intelligently used by activists, actually transform the nature of the processes themselves.

But before we all get too excited it is worth remembering that the net is not antithetical to consumerism, the misuse of labour or the free market. After all, the science fiction writer William Gibson invented the term 'cyberspace' to describe virtual reality in a future dominated by corporations who prey on a vast underclass. While the net does indeed benefit weaker, smaller actors, its impact is as yet far from universal.

Digital third worlds

The widely varying estimates of internet penetration make astonishing reading. The growth rate of internet access is more rapid than that of electricity, telephones, radios or televisions. In the developed world, around 25% of the adult population has access to the internet at the time of writing, and the majority of the population is expected to have access within five years.

Such figures invariably cite developed countries and this can easily disguise the fact that access to the net is, in global terms, still restricted to the privileged few. Worldwide, less than 2% of the world's population is online. For the most part, those who do have access to the internet are located in North America, Europe and Asia–Pacific. Across all regions of the world, we see that internet users have a higher than average personal income, and a high level of education and literacy when compared with their off-line neighbours.

The more the UK government and governments elsewhere continue to plan the future possibilities of online democracy and online education without addressing the imbalance of access, the more likely it is that many people lacking access will soon be locked out of the political and educational process. Not only will they be left out at the receiving end, but their protesting voices won't be heard online because those who lack access to the internet are also unable to produce and disseminate their own content there.

The picture *is* gradually changing. For example, all South American nations and about two-thirds of all African nations have at least some internet connectivity. Trade unions and charities are keen to give computer equipment and training to deserving groups. If an impoverished group can persuade a better-funded organization to donate a modem to connect to the telephone and can obtain a reliable telephone line – often the most difficult part – it can make contact with millions of people worldwide via international computer networks.

> Trade unions and charities are keen to give computer equipment and training to deserving groups.

The growth in free Internet Service Providers (ISPs) like FreeServe has meant that one barrier to access – the monthly subscription charge – has been removed, although that still leaves telephone bills to be paid and the cost of personal computers (PCs) to be met. Some countries are tackling this problem by providing free public access terminals in libraries, council offices and universities.

Where online access is impossible for local peoples, the internet can still bring to the attention of the world their concerns. The EcoNews Africa site (www.web.net/~econews/) is an example of this use. EcoNews Africa is an NGO coalition that monitors development issues from an African perspective. The site has been used to highlight the way the Masai of Tanzania have lost their land through the government backed growth in commercial farming enterprises, mining and tourism. At one point the Masai were threatened with eviction by a general management plan of the Ngorongoro Conservation Area Authority. The story was heard around the world; donors and individuals began to ask questions and put pressure on the Authority.

One of the largest networks and umbrella groups for online activism, information and support is the San Francisco-based Association for Progressive Communications (APC) (www.apc.org) – a coalition of computer networks providing services to over 25,000 activists and organizations in more than 130 countries.

The Institute of Global Communications (IGC) is one of the founding members of the APC. The IGC networks – PeaceNet, EcoNet, ConflictNet and LabourNet – together with APC partner networks claim to comprise the world's only computer communications system dedicated solely to environmental preservation, peace and human rights. We shall return to umbrella organizations in Chapter 2.

Netwars

One of the first uses of the net for political activism originated from the lead-up to the North American Free Trade Agreement in 1984. Diverse groups, from labour movements to feminists, to indigenous peoples and environmentalists, were campaigning against the threats posed by free trade. The net was used to establish contact between these groups not only to form a common front but also to understand the interrelationships between the issues which ranged from ethnic autonomy to international environmental standards.

A globalized networked capitalism requires a globalized and networked left response. Access to alternatives to official views of events is in itself a political phenomenon that is transforming the capacity of global civil society to build its own coalitions and networks and to link up in new and imaginative ways.

Participants in social conflicts are using the net to extend their struggles into cyberspace. Networking had been around for a long time before the advent of the internet, but the net is dramatically changing the way coalitions and networks can be built. Increasing access to electronic networks means that activists can easily link up, share experiences, disseminate and receive information, learn lessons from other struggles and discuss methods and tactics. The result of extending familiar and tested forms of political activism to cyberspace is critical in that it makes it much harder for the state to manage and counter.

The Rand report entitled 'CyberWar is Coming!' by national security analysts Arquilla and Ronfeldt formulated the concepts 'cyberwar' and 'netwar'. Cyberwar means the use of the net by the military to extend war through communication. Netwar refers to 'societal-level ideational conflicts waged in part through using the Internet as a mode of communication'.

The authors illustrate how 'advocacy movements [are] increasingly organising into cross-border networks and coalitions, identifying more with the development of civil society [than with nation-states] and using advanced information and communications technologies to strengthen their activities'.

Ronfeldt emphasizes that 'some of the heaviest users of the new communications networks and technologies are progressive, centre-left, and social activists [who work on] human rights, peace, environmental, consumer, labour, immigration, racial and gender-based issues'.

IRC [Internet Relay Chat] stepped into the limelight in early 1991, due to the Persian Gulf War. During the bombing of Iraq, hundreds of users from all over the world gathered on a single channel for live reports from users logged in from the Middle East.

INTERNET UNLEASHED

It's not hard to understand why activist groups are choosing to engage in netwar. Never before has a tiny organization with just a single PC, modem and telephone line been able to make its case to millions of people around the world.

'The important trend', messaged Michael Newman on the WELL (a pioneering online information service at www.well.com), 'is technology abetting the grassroots distribution of information rather than the information being the domain of huge institutions to dole out according to their agendas. The many-to-many model is going to eat the few-to-many model alive'.

All information wants to be free

The internet has been playing an increasingly important role in international politics. One highly significant application of the net has been to circumvent the informational controls imposed by authoritarian regimes or aggressors on their citizens.

> A single PC and telephone line allowed over 150 people to send e-mail out of Sarajevo in a three-month period.

It has also played in important role in recent and ongoing conflicts. During the siege of Sarajevo, when citizens risked death just by going out to try and buy food, telephones did not work and letters were undelivered, a few managed to get messages out to family overseas through the internet. A single PC and telephone line allowed over 150 people to send e-mail out of Sarajevo in a three-month period. In the former Yugoslavia, ZaMir ('for peace') – an electronic mail network dedicated to bringing together peace-orientated people, NGOs and the independent media – played a vital role. As the war destroyed the communication infrastructure, ZaMir (www.foebud.org/org/zamir/index.html) attempted to link local groups and activists to the outside world via the internet. Their letters service enabled refugees who had no computers, both those within the former Yugoslavia and those who had gone to other countries, to send and receive messages from relatives and friends locally and all over the world. Community e-mail centres were set up in order for volunteers to send e-mails to other volunteers who would then print them out and send them on by ordinary mail or fax. This way letters could be sent overnight from Zagreb to Belgrade and vice versa.

The net has also provided a way for independent commentary to be broadcast at times of political instability or crisis, as the excerpt below from an e-mail sent during an attempted coup in Russia demonstrates.

> *Moscow is full of tanks and military machines ... They try to close all mass media, they stopped CNN an hour ago ...*
> *Maybe you'd write me what do they say on your [American] TV about the situation, as we can't watch CNN now ... The best thing is to know that we aren't alone.*

International protest

From the UK to Brazil protest groups are planning political resistance via the net. E-mail can be a powerful tool for outreach and spreading information. A simple keystroke or a single click of the mouse, and you reach thousands of people, almost instantaneously.

The work of Citizens Against Police Brutality (COPB) displays how powerful the internet can be for grass-roots groups. In 1996, Le Drapeau Noir (www.multimania.com/zebwis/cops.htm), a group of

Swiss-based activists, began planning a worldwide International Day Against Police Brutality. At the same time in Montreal, Canada, COPB learned of the Swiss group's plan and decided to participate and to initiate an online outreach effort to involve other human rights organizations in this event.

COPB decided to set up an e-mail exchange list with these groups to share ideas and information. Included within this list were prisoners' rights groups, human rights activists, anti-fascist and anti-racism groups. What these diverse organizations had in common was firsthand experience with police brutality.

Using the well-known adage – 'act local, affect global' – participating organizations organized events within their own geographical areas but used the net to communicate daily with other groups across the world. No specific date was given for the international day until in late November COBP sent out an e-mail alert announcing the global demonstration and asking for groups wishing to participate to let them know. The following January, hundreds of simultaneous protest events took place around the world.

Labour movement

In 1972, no less a person than one of the founders of ARPANET, Charles Levinson, wrote a book entitled *International Trade Unionism* (now out-of-print) in which he advocated an international labour computer communications network.

At the time, Levinson was head of the international trade secretariat for the chemical workers, the Geneva-based ICF. He believed computerized 'data banks' could be linked by telex to ICF headquarters and from this information rapidly transmitted to affiliates. Within a few years, this vision was realized not with telexes but using the internet.

Most of the labour movement has been a great deal slower to recognize the opportunities generated by the net, but today the majority of unions have websites and make extensive use of e-mail to communicate with members, other unions and social justice groups across the world.

The net, then, is transforming virtually every aspect of activism. In the rest of this book, we'll provide examples of the myriad ways in which different types of activist groups – from mainstream political parties to the smallest campaign organizations – are using the internet to dramatically increase their effectiveness. And in the final two chapters, we'll explain how you can join them.

Other links

Acción Zapatista: www.utexas.edu/ftp/student/nave
Guerrillas in Mexico: www.onr.com/user/questad.html
Zapatista Net: www.actlab.utexas.edu:80/~zapatistas/

2 Red, Green and Radical Politics

Lawrence Grossman wrote in his book *The Electronic Republic* (Penguin, 1996) that the internet is set to have vast repercussions on the political agenda, perhaps to the extent of causing a reversal of political power, that top-down politics will be replaced by more people-orientated, democratic, bottom-up politics.

While that vision may have a way to go yet, it's certainly true that the net is empowering political groups to challenge government. The development of communication technology *is* reshaping our political processes. Cyberspace has the capacity through its generic means of free expression to give voices to those who would not normally have a voice in either national or international political affairs. Fringe groups are increasingly going online, especially when they are excluded from the mainstream political process or by the media.

What constitutes political action, and whether the internet actually widens civic participation in politics, are two questions that as yet remain unanswered. It is clear that the internet is a

> The net is
> empowering
> political groups to
> challenge
> government.

valuable tool for individuals who are already motivated by an interest in politics. For these people the net presents untold ways to campaign, lobby and pressure governments and engage in the mainstream political process. The internet, as borne out by many a political newsgroup, offers a forum to share experiences, pool knowledge, shape strategies and make a local concern an international one.

But does the net encourage individuals who would normally shy away from politics to get involved? Certainly it has the capacity to engage people who may have felt excluded from a hierarchical process, offering a flatter more democratic way of political engagement. Another question which we need to consider is whether online activism assists with face-to-face activism or instead creates armchair activists unable to translate the words they use in cyberspace into physical action.

Umbrella organizations

There are two large umbrella organizations, which we touched on in Chapter 1, providing the online infrastructure for red, green and radical political groups: the Association for Progressive Communications (APC) and the Institute of Global Communications (IGC), itself a member of the APC.

The IGC provides forums and web servers for women's, race and green issues as well as more mainstream political activism. The PeaceNet, EcoNet, ConflictNet and LabourNet networks within IGC each have bulletin boards, list servers and websites. For example, the Left List is a discussion forum concerned with creating fundamental social change, information and discussion on the various strands of the anarchist movement as well as multi-cultural news.

The IGC includes the Interpress service, a non-profit organization which ranks in the UNESCO top ten news agencies with over 900 outlets worldwide and reporting on news from all over the developing world. IGC regional news services include Central America updates, Nicanet weekly news and the Haiti Bulletin – publishing uncensored news from the country. In Africa, there is Info-Zaire and South Africa Watch amongst others. In the Middle East, there is Leb-Net Digest from the Lebanon and the Other Front which provides alternative reports on Israeli–Palestinian matters.

The left side of the net

The technological changes taking place worldwide are far reaching. Not since the Gutenberg press have we witnessed such a revolutionary change in the way information is disseminated, but these changes are creating new social divisions.

The ground for organizing the class struggle is shifting; there are new dangers of prolonged joblessness, globalization, repression and war. But there are also new opportunities for resistance and change that require new approaches to strategy, tactics and methods of organization.

Most left sites on the web are pretty passive affairs. The organized political left is on the net, but unlike the mainstream parties does not have the money or membership to make a big song and dance about it. Rather than act as a point for recruitment, lobbying or campaigning, the majority of left sites are not set up to offer much more than information, although many are linked to the more active labour movement and direct action sites which we will discuss in later chapters.

Activists will find these sites useful for resources, education and the many good links they support, but with few exceptions using them as a model for website design is not a fruitful idea. It is sad to say, but the big political sites of the Labour Party (www.labour.org.uk) in the UK and the Democrats in the USA are better models in terms of the innovations they have introduced to catch a browser's eye. Equally sadly, the propensity the various strands of the political left have for dividing and attacking each other is just as prevalent online.

One activist site (Internet Unleashed) has published guidelines for online political activists in the form of ten rules which we have summarized below:

> Most left sites on the web are pretty passive affairs.

1. Decide what issues are worthy of your time and be discriminating.

2. Do not assume you will need to work within a traditional group in order to be active.

3. Be realistic about the results you can gain.

4. Know the tools of the internet effectively.

5. Do not be intrusive or rude.

6. Write for the medium – it is different from other methods of publication.

7. Tell the truth.

8. Do not flame, and turn flaming to your advantage.

9. Provide ways for people to take action.

10. Do not forget to communicate with the media.

The Young Communist League (YCL) in the USA has one of the exceptions to most of the rather sparse websites on the left; perhaps knowing what they are up against with mainstream political sites has been an incentive to make this a lively site. The site contains regular updates on actions, an online page on how to build your own YCL club, a fun section and a simple online method for joining or donating funds.

Across the border it seems other comrades are just as well organized. The Communist Party of Canada (CPC) has both an English and French website; the English version's low bandwidth means access is slow but the site is well worth a visit to see how the net can work. It has a membership area which hosts online discussions, and the public information available is well worth looking at. The CPC message board divides postings into various categories, from solidarity-only to demonstration, to short notice and critical action, giving the e-mail address of the organizer and a short synopsis of the action.

The ANC (www.anc.org.za) website, as befits a party in power, has also taken a leaf out of the US campaigning bible with a site which links to the Mandela and Mbeki homepages and some online fund-raising such as posters and T-shirts. It also explains how to support the Mandela Millennium Fund.

One of the best sources of links for socialist and labour movement issues across the world is the UK-based Labour Left Briefing (www.briefing.org.uk). Be warned: this site's excellent and comprehensive links may cause hours of browsing!

Another site hosting comprehensive links is Jay's Leftist and Progressive Internet Resource Directory (www.nevaut.com/left1). It's a site we have returned to often for up-to-date information and an incredible range of links. As well as the links section, which is truly enormous and well put together, there are reviews of movies, articles and columns, a section on the news published by the mainstream press and a featured left website of the week.

There are many socialist and left 'web-rings' where groups and parties with similar aims have got together. When you visit one of the websites in the ring, you'll find a link to a list of all the others. We have included some of these on the CD accompanying this book.

List servers (or listservs) are another source of information on the left. Arm the spirit (http://burn.ucsd.edu/~ats) offers a listserv called ats2 which covers national liberation and anti-capitalism issues. Kurd1 is a list server for the Kurdistani struggle, and if you feel your mailbox is not full enough then join the Marxism mailing list – though you may wish to consider the digest version as posts come thick and fast!

The net may have the potential to help to create new and more democratic political systems, but it is only a tool: it is up to the individuals and groups involved to see that this happens. Certainly it opens channels so peoples from across a country or continent can form groups with similar political aims and interests. It breaks down the geographical barriers so virtual political parties do not have to be national but can be international, something of great relevance to socialism. It means both membership and activism can be pursued on a global level.

While there are hundreds of radical US websites, only a few stand out as providing useful information, links and commentary. The best we've found are the Communist Party USA and The Socialist, the official publication of the Socialist Party USA.

Another good example is Resistance, an Australian socialist youth organization in solidarity with the Democratic Socialist Party.

Reference sources

International Viewpoint (www.internationalen.se/sp/ivp.htm).
Founded by the Marxist economist Ernest Mandel (1923–95), *International Viewpoint* is an international news and analysis magazine published monthly by the socialist world movement known as The Fourth International.

Soman's Revolutionary Socialist Links Page (www.geocities. com/CapitolHill/1884). A great set of pages, divided into many categories and with over 800 links.

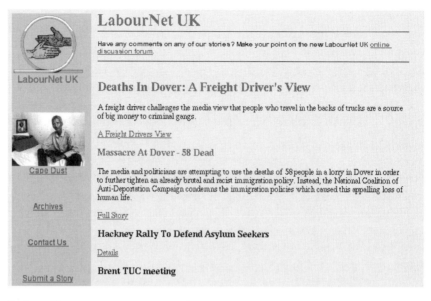

LabourNet

British Progressive Links (www.psr.keele.ac.uk). A comprehensive directory of radical and progressive websites in Britain.

Stec's Commie-Pinko Homepage (www.geocities.com/CapitolHill/7078). Links to anarchist, socialist, communist and progressive websites on the web.

Green Left Weekly (www.greenleft.org.au). Australia's leading red-green newspaper. Some of the best left-wing coverage of world events. Many articles of interest to socialists and environmentalists, feminists and international solidarity activists.

LEFTforum (http://members.tripod.com/~leftforum). *LEFTforum* is an online socialist journal which wants to facilitate and inform socialist and left-wing debate, discussion and activity.

The Marxists Internet Archive (MIA) (www.marxism.org). Created in 1998, the MIA provides comprehensive information on the history of Marxism and Marxist writers and reference material.

The Real History Archives (www.webcom.com/~lpease/index.htm). Contains information on conspiracies and political 'no-goodings' throughout the world; it is a well-organized site with easily accessible information.

Anarchy

Anarchy and the various anarchist movements have found a natural home on the web. Ironically, perhaps, anarchist groups are among the most organized political groupings on the net. According to Ronfeldt's thesis, this makes perfect sense. Who better to exploit a system that 'erodes hierarchy' and requires the co-ordination of decentralized, autonomous groups in co-operative action than anarchists and libertarian socialists?

It is no coincidence that anarchists and libertarian socialists on the web are at the forefront of issues concerning net privacy and censorship. We shall look in more detail at some of the proactive anarchist sites later in the book.

The proliferation of anarchist sites on the web has resulted in regular attacks by government. In Italy, the Carabiniere's Anti-Crime Special Operations Group has raided the homes of a number of activists, many in the anarchist movement. They confiscated journals, magazines, pamphlets, diaries and videotapes. They also took personal computers, one of which hosted BITS Against the Empire, a node of Cybernet and Fidonet networks.

In the United Kingdom, a number of computer networks have been attacked. The Terminal Boredom bulletin board system in Scotland was shut down allegedly after police had arrested a hacker who was affiliated with the bulletin board.

To learn more about anarchist theory you could do worse than taking a look at The Anarchist Archive (http://flag.blackened. net/index.html). There are also a few online courses for studying anarchy. The Anarchy and the Internet course promises to get you net savvy as well as doing wonders for your political education. Spunk (www.spunk.org) is an independent anarchist publishing project which collates anarchy information from around the world both online and off-line. It has a good list of links to other anarchy sites and produces downloadable flyers in various European languages.

> Anarchy [has] found a natural home on the web.

Other anarchist sites

The Situationists International Archive: www.nothingness.org
Terra y Libertad: www.geocities.com/CapitolHill/2374
Anti capital web: www.webcom.com/maxang
Black Flag: http://flag.blackened.net/blackflag/

Burn: http://burn.ucsd.edu/
Decadent Action: www.underbelly.demon.co.uk/decadent/
Emma Goldman Papers Project: http://sunsite.berkeley.edu/goldman/
General Strike Page: http://www.dnai.com/~figgins/generalstrike/
Industrial Workers of the World: www.iww.org
Luddites online: www.Luddites.com
Mid Atlantic Infoshop: www.infoshop.org
Anarcha-feminism: http://burn.ucsd.edu/~mai/afem_kiosk.html
Anarchy Ireland: www.geocities.com/CapitolHill/4716/
Anarchist Federation (UK): http://burn.ucsd.edu/~acf/
Anarchist FAQ Web: www.geocities.com/CapitolHill/1931/
Anarchist Yellow Pages: www.tao.ca/lake/

Green

We will take a closer look at green movement sites in Chapter 5. There are, along with more direct green political actions, a number of sites on the web dedicated to green politics such as the Green Parties of North America (www.greens.org) site. This site has perhaps the most comprehensive green resources on the net. It has listings and contacts for organizations across the USA and a good international links section.

The California Green Party Information Clearing-house (www. deepthought.armoury.com/~geoffg/greens/greens/) is one of the most successful green state organizations. Their site offers a party platform, brochure text and membership information and listings.

In the UK, the Green Party of England and Wales site (www.greenparty.org.uk) is not such a good read. It contains a good directory of green councillors and numerous press releases put out by the party but little more of interest at the time of writing, unlike the Scottish green site (www.Scottishgreens. org.uk) which is a plethora of information and contains good links to other green parties across the world.

The far right

One of the prices paid for the freedom of speech to be found on the net is that it provides a forum for far right groups to spread hate messages. The number of fascist, nazi and race-hate groups on the web has grown significantly in the past few years. It has been estimated that in the USA the number leapt from 167 in 1997 to 537 in 1998.

In Germany, neo-nazi groups have set up bulletin board systems to establish links across the western world with other nazi or fascist groups. These are used to co-ordinate activities such as rallies and demonstrations in other countries (such actions are banned in Germany), to spread propaganda, alert sympathizers, recruit and raise money.

Anti Fascist Web (www.antifacist.org) uses the internet to alert browsers to fascist action across the world. As well as posting alerts, the site hosts a subscriber information bulletin. Some of the anti-fascist groups are difficult to keep track of; often their sites are subject to attack from fascist groups. Two sites well worth visiting are Nazism Exposed which tracks fascist groups on the net and A Guide to Hate Groups on the Internet. Anti Fascist Action combines action on the internet with real life action against fascists in the UK.

Although some of the hate groups may seem patently idiotic, one should never underestimate the power of the net to disseminate and communicate, and the lunatic fringe understands this. Enter the US Right Side of the Web, a land where elements such as Town Hall are slickly put together and at first browse do not appear to be anything more than a news story site for eccentric but harmless conservatives. But enter a chatroom and you are assaulted with deranged viewpoints like discussions on how best to execute homosexuals.

The National Alliance seems to have problems with using any other word but Aryan. The pages are well designed, with audio if you want to listen to some of their vitriolic spewings. Church and State is a far right website with its own brand of Christianity which includes hatred for just about everyone but themselves. Stormfront is the home of the American Nazi Party. There is even an Aryan dating society.

People for the American Way (PFAW) publishes Right Wing Watch Online, a free electronic newsletter on the Religious Right political movement. The site includes an archive of past issues as well as other information on right-wing religious groups that use the political process to impose their values on US citizens. PFAW also maintains a library that archives the movement's political

> One should never underestimate the power of the net to disseminate and communicate.

propaganda, including videos of television and radio broadcasts, direct mail, newsletters and books.

Other sites

Anti Facist Resource Page: www.geocities.com/CapitolHill/Senate/5602/index2.html
Nazism Exposed: www.ekran.no/html/nazismexposed/
Anti-Facist Action online: www.geocities.com/CapitolHill/Senate/5602/index2.html
Fight Racism Fight Fascism: www.geocities.com/Capitol Hill/1320/
Hate on the web: www.vir.com/Shalom/hate/

Advocacy and pressure groups

UK Labour Party

Socialist Campaign Group News (www.poptel.org.uk/scgn). Published monthly under the auspices of the Campaign Group of labour MPs.

Tribune (www.abel.net.uk/~rost2000.tribune). Online version of the weekly newspaper that sometimes supports the Labour Party.

Fabian Society (www.fabian-society.org.uk). Blairite and right wing, they describe themselves as 'the UK's premier think tank and democratic membership organisation'.

Labour Co-ordinating Committee (LCC) (-http://dispace.dial.pipex.com). Blairite, New Labour, the LCC is a network of constituency Labour Party activists who are committed to modernization and whatever that may mean.

Labour Reform. Campaigning for a more democratic and accountable Labour Party.

General

Campaign for Press and Broadcasting Freedom (www.cpbf.demon.co.uk/). An anti-censorship organization.

Charter 88 (www.charter88.org.uk). A UK organization working for electoral reform and democracy, their site features a central lobby providing up-to-date parliamentary bulletins and commentary as well as information and links on freedom of information, addresses of local groups, searchable archives and publications. The site is well designed and easy to navigate with a good 'Take action' section. The site provides a link to Charter 88's recently launched Citizen21 website. Again, this is a well-designed site offering an online service for educators on freedom of information, Bill of Rights and voting reform.

Statewatch (www.poptel.org.uk/statewatch). A UK-based organization that monitors state and civil liberties in Europe, with a good section on Northern Ireland.

Political prisoners

There are many sites in support of political prisoners around the world. However, these sites tend to disappear and reappear regularly and one can never be sure a url will get you there.

As well as sites for individual prisoners such as the Free Geronimo Plat there is the Solidarity Group for Political Prisoners, and for further information on political prisoners take a look at Equal Justice USA (www.quixote.org/ej/) and the various free Mumia Abu Jamal sites (www.mumia.org and www.freemumia.org).

Refuse and Resist is an American-based website fighting the political and ideological programmes of America. A recent entry to the site contained a stark red message that read 'Do you think critics of government should be sentenced to death for political beliefs?' after which a message flashed up about Mumia Abu Jamal who at the time of writing had just received a warrant of execution.

Other political prisoner sites

Death Penalty Information Centre: www.deathpenaltyinfo.org
Free Alvaro Now!: http://members.tripod.com/~defensa
Free Jimmy Segura (Soledad prisoner): www.silverload.net/freejimmy

Free Leonard Peltier Support Group: www.freepeltier.org
Justice Net: www.igc.org/justice
Political Prisoner Campaigns: http://burn.ucsd.edu/~udb/cmpp-alvaro.html

Euroscepticism

Euroscepts have created a textbook example of how political groups [...] can use the web as a political tool.

In the UK, Eurosceptics have created a textbook example of how political groups, outside the mainstream, can use the web as a political tool. Dozens of Eurosceptics have seized the advantage with lively and sometimes quirky homepages that are more engrossing than the European Union's comparatively dry and bureaucratic homepages. Among the interesting things the Eurosceptics have done have been to describe horror stories involving Eurocrats, ridicule designs for the new Euro coin, broadcast 'No to the EU' in nearly a dozen languages and produce analytical material on the dangers of the Euro. Well worth a look for ideas in terms of how to design an effective web presence.

3 Towards a Global Labour Net

Britain's largest trade union, Unison (www.unison.org.uk), was the first trade union in the world to offer free internet access to its members.

In Canada, unions have created 'Buy Union' (www.clc-ctc.ca/buy-union/) advice pages with lists of union-organized companies broken down by product and geographical region.

LabourNet (www.labournet.net) provided information to the TTGS (telecomunication taskforce group for general strike) when 1000 dockers, threatened by the army and federal police, marched through Santos, Brazil chanting the slogan 'Santos, Liverpool, Seoul, Amsterdam, the same world, the same struggle'.

During ABC's lock-out of Disney workers activists posted protest notices on the ABC web pages recipe section.

In Sweden, unions bulk-buy computer hardware to help boost the number of trade unions online, selling computers to members at up to 30% off retail cost.

In Britain, the General and Municipal Boilermakers Union (GMB) (www.gmb.org.uk) has negotiated with British Gas Services (now Transco) an agreement for mobile teleworking, which allows shop stewards to communicate with each other and with members through the Transco network.

The 20 million-strong International Federation of Chemical, Energy, Mining and General Workers Unions (www.icem.org) was

> Shop stewards [can] communicate with each other and with members through the Transco network.

the first union to launch a 'cyberpicket' of a multinational company: tyre giant Bridgestone/Firestone. On 12 July 1994, 4200 members of the United Steel Workers Association (USWA) (www.uswa.org) went on strike at the US Bridgestone/Firestone plant. The company had wanted to eliminate the joint labour management committees for employee involvement and reduce the effective grievance procedures and seniority protection. In response, together with ICEM and the Industrial Union Department of the American Federation of Labor and Congress of Industrial Organizations (AFL/CIO), USWA launched an internet-based global campaign.

ICEM used its website to alert members and to call for solidarity. One of the campaign aims was to generate unfavourable media coverage for the company. To this end the website published the e-mail addresses of the company and its subsidiaries throughout the world, as well as the e-mail addresses of its top executive and the names of major shareholders. In some cases, the union provided links to the shareholders' own websites and urged affiliate unions and sympathizers to send e-mail messages. ICEM believes the net was integral to the successful outcome of USWA's action.

Through the net, information is processed rapidly and at low cost, allowing unions to link together in international solidarity. It makes the activities of multinationals and transnationals more transparent, exposing the links between factory closures in Europe and growing sweatshops in Asia. Many internet commentators believe the labour movement can establish permanent web pages that monitor multinationals' codes of conduct. The net is having a profound effect on how the labour movement mobilizes and communicates.

Debate, discussion and organizing are vital to the labour movement. Unions have traditionally organized vocally, through speeches and meetings. Printing has also been used to produce magazines, leaflets and position papers, and now the internet offers a huge array of ways to organize in the digital age. There are bulletin boards, e-mails giving details of urgent actions, cyberpicket lines, distance learning sites, information websites, e-zines, newsgroups and chatrooms specifically set up to discuss labour issues.

The AFL/CIO (www.aflcio.org) mentioned above has made many innovative uses of its web pages. Executive Paywatch (www.aflcio.paywatch.org/index.html) lets browsers work out how long it would take to match the salaries paid by corporate leaders. Pay Gap is a calculator that lets women find out how long it would take them to make up the pay gap between themselves and male workers. If that isn't depressing enough, with a click of the mouse you can find out what you could have bought with the money you didn't earn – including servings of macaroni…

Yet, although the labour movement has been built on the principle of solidarity, and hence is an ideal candidate for co-operation on a global network, the internet as a tool for promoting and organizing solidarity on a local, national and international level was, with a few exceptions, not really recognized until the early 1990s. Indeed, early suspicion of the net may well have hampered the development of labour movement activism.

Ironically, it has been the emergence of new corporations and the process of increasing globalization that has created the impetus for the labour movement's launch into cyberspace. As e-commerce becomes ever more sophisticated, the need for the labour movement to find imaginative and innovative ways to combat those who seek to exploit workers and diminish their rights becomes ever more important.

For corporations, the net is not only a tool for selling themselves to a mass market, increasingly it is used by transnationals to keep on top of developments in national and international economies and to monitor the political and industrial stability in the regions in which they operate. The net allows companies to increase production within a decreased timeframe and ultimately this is changing the structures of companies and how they treat their workforces. It raises diverse issues: isolation of workers through increased teleworking, increasing redundancy through streamlining of work, decline in working conditions and – ultimately – greater unemployment.

Unions need to use the same tools as capitalists in order to fight back on behalf of their members. Using computer communications to strengthen and build the labour movement across the globe is one way forward. Fundamentally, unions are networks, and the internet is the largest and perhaps the most important network in existence. As a tool, it has enormous potential to get people communicating and building networks of shared interests. By the very nature of the net, these networks need to be built on new horizontal channels of communications as opposed to the traditional structures of trade unions. Today, any union member with access to a PC and modem can discuss strategy and action instantaneously with colleagues across the world.

Rob's Labour Links (www.netcore.ca/~rspring) is a site with links to other sites of interest for labour activists. The main concentration of links are to Canadian resources, primarily those located in Ontario, but other geographic locations have been included.

A little history

As we mentioned in Chapter 1, Charles Levinson was perhaps the first proponent of organizing workers via the internet. He envisaged a system which would combine electronic databases with telex to inform trade unions throughout the world about corporate actions. But it was over a decade before the labour movement used the internet in any strategic manner.

Although many local branches of unions in the USA and Canada had quietly been exchanging information throughout the early 1980s on electronic bulletin boards it was not until 1986 that the American Federation of Musicians in New York became the first US union to go online.

The same year saw the creation of the Canadian SoliNet by Marc Belanger for the Canadian Union of Public Employees (CUPE) (www.labornet.org/labornet/unions.html).

SoliNet was founded to create 'a sense of community among CUPE locals by providing them with news information and support' and has become a model for other trade unions keen to get online. It has been used for strike support and for transferring leaflets from trade union public relations departments to negotiators in the field.

The 1989 caretakers strike in Hope, British Columbia is an early example of SoliNet's effectiveness. SoliNet, hearing that a Hells Angels bikers convention was being held in Hope, invited the bikers to join the Hope picket line. News of this brought huge amounts of publicity to the caretakers' cause. Information on the state of negotiations was spread by the internet. The result was a swift end to the dispute and victory for the caretakers.

Another service offered by SoliNet is helping shop-stewards. Stewards can post messages into a closed conference asking for help from other members in finding solutions to their problems.

It was not until 1992 that SoliNet was joined on the web by an organization with similar resources. The Institute of Global Communications (IGC – see Chapter 2) helped to set up LabourNet (www.labournet.org), a network for unions and labour solidarity groups. LabourNet offers online conference facilities and bulletin boards as well as links to unions, news of strikes, notification of events and appeals for solidarity. There are now affiliated LabourNets in the UK (www.labournet.net), Canada and Australia.

In the UK the Labour Telematics Centre (LTC) (www.labourtel. org.uk) was established in January 1993. It was set up to give support to the labour movement through online communication and to encourage the use of telematics – computer-based communications and information technology. Part of its work includes development of bargaining databases and issues to do with the impact of telematics on employment and labour organization.

In 1995, Unison became the first UK union to set up a website. Prior to this, over 50 local Unison branches had used Poptel (www.poptel.org.uk) to communicate with each other through e-mail discussion. In 1999, as we mentioned at the beginning of the chapter, it also became the first union in the world to offer its members free net connections.

> Unison became the first UK union to set up a website.

Things have definitely improved from the early days of online labour activism when trade union websites seemed to be at a loss as to their purpose, offering little more than a picture of their president or secretary.

The Trades Union Congress (TUC) (www.tuc.org.uk) was one of the first national trade union centres in the world to create a website. It was innovative in allowing TUC workers to add their own pages to the site.

These days the majority of unions in the UK and around the world have websites, many of which are highly sophisticated. The net's strength as a powerful weapon for the labour movement in industrial campaigning has been recognized and increasingly utilized, as has alliance-building with other social movements. The way the net can spread information efficiently and rapidly also means that many actions that have been excluded from traditional news media can now be published with very effective results.

Trade unions on the net

It is estimated that some 4 million American trade unionists are online. In the UK, the number is much lower but growing fast. Although we are far from seeing an all-encompassing labour net, one cannot help but feel excited by how the net is currently used by the labour movement. We can categorize current use of the net into:

- political activism

- solidarity

- research and education.

Political activism

Union activists can use the net to run campaigns, swap strategies, discuss tactics and organize solidarity with other unions and social justice organizations throughout the world. The Speckled Bird (www.igc.apc.org/strike) site hosts a list of industrial actions around the world. By clicking on a particular strike action, the user is routed to the website of the union involved and can read more about the action. The Cyber-Picket Line (www.cf.ac.uk/ccin/union) site gives daily updates on union actions and what users can do to help.

Leaflets can be posted on the web with a download facility so they can be printed out with graphics. They can also be produced so they can be changed on the web, enabling local branches to customize literature to suit their own needs.

Possibly the first national industrial dispute in which a union used the internet as a matter of course was the US Teamsters strike in United Parcel Services (UPS). The Teamsters' website carried daily UPS updates that could be read online or downloaded, photocopied and distributed to members. This format was also used for flyers and press releases. The site also recruited volunteers and shared news of support.

However, it was the 1995 Liverpool dockers' strike that was fundamental in influencing trade union activism on the net. In many ways the dockers' strike broke the mould in the way trade unions organize during strikes. Ironically, it was the lack of support given to the dockers by their own union that drove them to seek solidarity from other sources, and in doing so they linked what was happening to them to the wider concerns of dockers throughout the world. From erosion of workers' rights and working conditions to how globalization impacts on the environment and human rights in general, the Liverpool dockers recognized that a globalised commerce requires a globalized workers' response.

Through the use of internet-facilitated communications a strike that started with 500 dockers grew to include thousands of supporters. GreenNet (www.gn.apc.org), the UK wing of the Association for Progressive Communications, offered a free website, and LabourNet supplied on-the-spot reports from Liverpool. One of the side-effects of using computer-aided and international effort on many of the dockers involved was that they used their redundancy payments to set up a workers' enterprise to train themselves and others in new technology.

Information is everything during a strike. By using the net to spread information rapidly and widely and to engage in discussion, the dockers were able to co-ordinate two international Days of Action, to organize international conferences and to raise much needed fighting funds. Picket lines were organized in ports across the world, and ships were not permitted to dock at American ports as longshoremen refused to cross picket lines set up by local support groups. The internet had facilitated the communication and discussion that led to all these actions.

> Picket lines were organized in ports across the world.

Solidarity

The internet is increasingly used by unions during industrial actions to seek e-mail solidarity. This can take the form of an Action Alert on the website asking unions and individuals to e-mail the strikers with messages of support, or perhaps to e-mail the companies involved, in protest. In the USWA action, Bridgestone/Firestone admitted that they had to set up a parallel e-mail system as e-mails from union supporters were clogging up the company's system.

The dockers' strike and the resulting global action helped facilitate a general acknowledgement that workers' rights are rooted in a broader understanding of the place of workers in society as a whole. An important development facilitated by the internet is the labour movement's increasing engagement with non-unions working towards equal rights, environmental and human rights issues. Cyberspace links have been established with consumer groups, indigenous peoples' movements, educators and anti-poverty groups all over the world.

International issues such as Nike and the Clean Clothes Campaign have involved not only grass-roots campaigners but unions with similar objectives. The internet has been integral to both.

Research and education

The internet represents the biggest library in the world, and its section on the labour movement, although a little disjointed, is vast and informative. Many websites act as information clearing houses. Along with LabourNet, the best places to look for links for research activists include Labour Left Briefing in the UK and for global links Jay's Leftist and Progressive Links. The net means that unions in the south can compare wage structures with comparative work in the north.

LabourStart (www.labourstart.org) is a service provided by Labour and Society International for the international trade union movement. The site offers many services to unions and provides a wealth of information and links. Unlike some sites, it is updated daily and very easy to navigate. It includes an international calendar of labour events, an urgent action section and news on strikes around the world – including what you can do to support strikes via the internet. There is a labour webmasters forum, details of labour radio and TV web-casts and a free e-mail facility.

Online learning enables people to study wherever they are located and at their own time and speed. Many networks and unions are developing distance learning facilities on their websites. SoliNet has linked their educational work with local universities in order to provide access courses for trade unionists.

Barriers to access

There are still major barriers to labour activism on the net, not least in terms of expense. In particular, equipment costs seriously hamper access in the developing world. In some countries, access is limited to business and government or censored by the state. A further difficulty comes from general levels of education amongst blue-collar workers in many developing countries, who lack the computer literacy necessary to make effective use of the technology.

Charley Lewis of the Congress of South African Trade Unions (COSATU) (www.cosatu.org.za/) South Africa said:

> *I look at my own country, where the majority of the population cannot even read and write, much less launch Pegasus Mail. In these kinds of contexts, the challenge of information literacy takes on a whole new meaning. Where most people lack even the basic tools of the industrial age one is almost tempted to ask how we dare even contemplate the information age.*

Yet the benefits of being online for movements in the south are manifold, not least of which is the ability to seek out the truth as opposed to government and commercial propaganda. More of this in Chapter 6.

Despite the problems of internet access that exist, union internet activity is confined neither to labour in the more advanced OECD economies nor to the technically-based unions within those countries. With the aid of networks in the west, labour networks are being established in Africa. South Africa developed WorkNet in 1987. Glasnet in Russia has provided conferences in both Russian and English. Glasnet states the purpose of its site is to 'provide unions and other users on the net with electronic forums to exchange information and to discuss various labour-related issues'. KAS-KOR considers computer communications vital to the reinvigoration of a labour movement.

The impact of the net on labour

The net is not, however, unqualified good news for the labour movement. Physical labour and industrial machinery are becoming less and less important when compared with information. In some fields, new computer-mediated technology means fewer workers, less resources and lower wages.

Marxist economist Vojin Dakovic in his book *Anti-Capital* argues that cybernetics and automation will bring about the final stage of industrial capitalism. He states that by 'bringing unlimited quantities of cheaper labour … technology has set the stage for the final battle for capital on the world market'.

In April 1998 an online rights campaign was launched in Cardiff, Wales, by FIET (www.fiet.org) – an international white-collar union federation with affiliates in 120 countries. FIET's manifesto includes the right of free access by workers and unions to corporate e-mail systems and to trade union websites relevant to workers' rights. They further call for the prohibition of electronic monitoring of workers' e-mail by employers.

FIET identified teleworkers as being in the most danger from the downside of the new telecommunications. Teleworkers are often isolated, inadequately informed of developments in their companies and have very few employee rights.

The increasing and more sophisticated use of the internet by unions may also herald the advance of cyber union-busting by companies. For example, by spreading misinformation through the net about the reasons for industrial action, by denigrating unions through company websites and in some cases monitoring e-mail communication between union members. This reflects growing fears about censorship and privacy issues which we shall discuss in later chapters.

Although the net is the new frontier for union activity, it is not the answer to many current union problems – although it may help to stop the drain of members and may even recruit new members in white-collar work. Some of these issues have been highlighted by the founder of the excellent LabourStart website, Labour internet guru Eric Lee. Lee has written extensively about the use of the internet by the labour movement, and his writing provides a good place to start for anyone interested in these issues. Lee believes the current use of the net by the labour movement is far from fulfilling its potential and is still hampered by issues of access and education.

Many labour commentators foresee the day there will be a global labour net, others are more cautious, but none dismisses the relevancy of such a move. As globalization continues its march, it is essential for unions and labour movements to build international networks and links.

As the costs of technology decrease, it becomes easier for movements to go online but unless there is some co-ordination this amounts to tiny individual drops in a vast electronic ocean.

Databases need to be standardized in order for them to be accessed with greater ease from anywhere in the world. Software for translation must be adopted by more of the labour move-ment. For example, the Korean labour movement is very active

> It is essential for unions and labour movements to build international networks and links.

on the web but much of their information is in Korean. Translation programmes available to the average internet user such as Babelfish are very basic and unable to cope with complicated documents on collective bargaining.

Computer conferencing, as currently developed by LTC and other organizations, must continue to be developed. It is ideal for unions especially over large geographical areas, reducing costs because no money needs to be spent on travel, accommodation or venues, or providing opportunities to include more people, thereby generating a more democratic process. The use of e-mail discussions provides more time for consideration and can lead to fewer 'heat of the moment' responses.

Ronfeldt in 'Cyberwar is Coming!' states that 'institutions can be defeated by networks, and it may take networks to counter networks'. By establishing a global labour net, perhaps it will be possible for unions to counter the might of the transnationals?

We shall give the last word on how labour can use the net to the LabourStart site. 'If you think all there is to the Internet is email and the Web, you're missing what is perhaps the very best use trade unionists can make of the new communications technology: building online "virtual communities." Use these new tools like web forums and live chat to run solidarity campaigns, trade union education, distribute news and much more.'

Other sites

Solidarity: www.solidarity.com
Teamsters for a Democratic Union: www.igc.apc.org/tdu
Union resource network: www.unions.org
ICEM Cyber Campaign: www.icem.org
International Labour Organization: www.ilo.org
Jobs with Justice: www.igc.apc.org/jwj
Labour Left Briefing Links Page: http://links.briefing.org.uk
General strike page: www.dnai.com/~figgins/generalstrike
To find out more about SoliNet, refer to the CuPE homepage at www.cupe.ca/

4 | Non-profits and Charities

Throughout this chapter we shall refer to non-profit-making organizations and charities as NGOs (non-governmental organizations).

As we mentioned in Chapter 1, Peace Brigades International (PBI) has been using e-mail for some years, both to communicate with volunteers in the field and to alert members, supporters and the media to violations of human rights. PBI is not the only NGO which has been using internet technology in this way. Their main website provides links to membership offices in various countries across Europe and the USA and Canada. Sophistication and information varies between sites but to get a good flavour of how the internet can benefit a grass-roots NGO it is worth having a look at PBI's site.

NGOs are extremely diverse, ranging from huge internationals, such as Amnesty International (www.amnesty.org.uk) and Oxfam (oxfam.org.uk), through local groups concerned with neighbourhood advocacy to guerrilla organizations actively opposing governments. Many smaller NGOs have traditionally seen the net as something beyond their financial or technical reach, but as this chapter will show, even the smallest NGO can benefit.

NGOs such as Oxfam and Save the Children (www.savethe children.org) have had a presence on the internet for many years and have been using e-mail from the early 1980s, as it presents a cheap and extremely effective way to communicate with offices in remoter parts of the world. In more recent years, net use has been expanded to publicize human rights violations and environmental destruction, for local, national and global advocacy, for networking and collaboration with other NGOs and for raising funds. Amnesty International is at the forefront of harnessing the internet for gathering support and donations and publishing alerts on various campaigns across the globe. The Amnesty site is one of the best designed sites on the net and while many groups cannot afford the design and technology used by Amnesty, a lot of tips on website design and feature use can be picked up by a visit to the site.

Interestingly, the use NGOs make of the net has been taken more seriously by governments than by a lot of the NGOs themselves. A report published in 1995 by Charles Swett, an advisor for the US Department of Defense, entitled 'Strategic Assessment: the Internet', specifically singles out APC/IGC as one of the most important networks on the internet and one the US government should be concerned about for its effectiveness both in hosting NGOs and raising issues concerning governmental policy and human rights/environmental abuses.

Perhaps the most effective and long-term NGO use of the net has been in mailing lists and e-mail communication. For example, mailing lists are used by members of the UN non-governmental forums (www.un.org) to distribute UN conference and policy documents. NGOs use e-mail clearing houses to distribute information to members throughout the world and to organize international campaigns.

> Even the smallest NGO can benefit.

Cost

Any organization relying on donations needs to keep an eye on costs. The internet can cut down on paper, mailing, fax and telephone costs. Using the web for research can cut out expensive paper trails and the need to employ outside consultancies. Much information that traditionally had to be expensively printed and distributed can be posted on a website: annual reports, minutes, policy documents, calls for conference papers and results of conferences – all cutting down on costs.

Volunteer recruitment

A lot of work within medium and small NGOs is carried out by volunteers. For some this is a deliberate policy, for others purely cost driven. In either case, this can mean a high turnover of people and considerable time and resources invested in training. The net can help facilitate this process, offering ways for people to get active at both low and high levels of involvement.

For example, by placing FAQ (frequently asked questions) sheets and training information on the web, you can cut down on the time it would normally take to give inductions and to bring people up to speed on what your organization does. This can also help to get people motivated before they come to a training or volunteer information day.

The web can be used for the recruitment of volunteers, and there are sites to help you with this, from the US Impact Online (www.impactonline.org) site for advocacy groups, to Envirolink for volunteers to work on green and animal welfare issues. In the UK sites such as CharityNet do a similar job. Individual organizations such as Amnesty International, Peace Brigades International and Oneworld Online (www.oneworld.org) all have information or specific web pages on how to volunteer and what positions are available.

Impact Online links people interested in volunteering with organizations in need of volunteers. Activists looking for a volunteer opportunity can search the website by name of organization, area of interest and geographic area.

Impact Online also makes it possible for grass-roots groups without the resources to set up their own website to establish a presence on the web. NGOs can set up a free web page that includes contact information, a mission statement or description of the organization's purpose, and information on volunteer needs.

Community

The internet can also help grass-roots leaders organize information for the public. Neighborhoods Online (www.libertynet.org/nol/natl.htm) is a very good example of this. The site includes features on neighbourhood empowerment, community development, economic development, education and health and human services.

Advocacy

As we shall discuss in the following chapter, the web provides quick, cheap and efficient ways to mobilize people through action alerts, petitions and online media releases.

Service delivery

A website is one of the new and innovative ways that an NGO can deliver services. For example, the Tear Fund site allows you to sponsor an Indonesian child via the internet. Other sites such as the US Precious in His Sight (www.precious.org/) help place children for adoption and have an adoption photo-listing service on their website.

Research

The plethora of information available, from websites to newsgroups and bulletin boards, means the net can provide a very efficient way to keep up to date on issues related to your campaign or cause. Information can be downloaded straight onto your computer and disseminated across a network without incurring photocopying and paper expenses.

NetActivism (www.idealist.org) is a good site for many areas of interest for NGOs, as is the Canadian Charity Village (www.charityvillage.com), a huge site for non-profit resources. Whilst Canadian focused, it provides many useful articles and help for a broad range of non-profit issues that span the globe.

Publicity

On the net you can publicize your programmes, media campaigns, newsletters and even case-studies. Publishing on the web can generate huge media attention. A good site will be talked about by net-surfers, and by publicizing a website through traditional media you can attract a good deal of attention to your cause from very small ads or editorial copy.

Networking

Opportunities to build coalitions with other organizations are unparalleled. Whilst the net does not take away the need for face-to-face communication, it does offer cheap and effective ways to work with other organizations and members without the usual geographic and time barriers.

For example the Hunger Site (www.thehungersite.com) (which caused much debate as to its veracity in the early days but which is now accepted as a legitimate site) was set up and paid for by corporate sponsors. It asks visitors to click on the site once a day in order for a donation to be made by the corporate sponsors to the UN world food programme. The Hunger Site has facilitated discussions and information exchange on the causes and possible solutions to hunger, as well as providing education materials for use throughout the world.

Networking is, perhaps, currently the most effective way that NGOs can use the web. SeniorNet (www.seniornet.com), the San Francisco-based network with healthcare as its prime concern, has more than 10,000 individual subscribers.

The internet can facilitate partnership between organizations with respect to programme sharing and policy development. For example, OneWorld Online has an extremely diverse range of organizations in its partnership, ranging from human rights to sustainable development.

Structure

Finally, the net makes for flatter comunication. This means volunteers and members have more opportunity to feel involved and part of participatory decision making. Some voluntary organizations that run on federal global structures now use e-mail to make and take decisions, saving time and expense on meetings. This way local decisions can still be made but information can be spread across the organization and in line with global guidelines.

E-mail may not replace the need for face-to-face communication, but it can make this communication more effective in terms of decisions and time. Much can be discussed by e-mail prior to a meeting, sometimes making the meeting unnecessary, at other times diffusing likely tensions and often improving consensus-building processes.

Resources

CharityNet (www.charitynet.org) was set up by the UK Charities Aid Foundation (CAF) to provide a gateway to networking, discussion, fund-raising information, links and resources. There are links to the Charity Commission website which not only includes helpful information on setting up and running charities but a searchable database of registered UK charities and trusts.

www.idealist.org is wonderful for finding non-profit information. Although predominantly US focused, it provides links and information on government, finance, management, public relations and other issues of interest.

The Foundation Center (www.fdncenter.org) is one of the best sources for information on grants for organizations and individuals. Although again US focused, it has links and advice that are of great help to UK NGOs. Similarly with Foundations Online (www.fdn.org/grantmaker) and the Internet Non-profit Centre (www.nonprofit-info.org/) which is excellent for help on administration, personnel management and marketing for NGOs.

Action Without Borders (www.idealist.org) provides a huge and exhaustive web directory of non-profit resources, which is very easy to use and well worth a visit. Their FAQ sheets are wonderful for short but informative advice and help.

The NGO Café (www.soc.itech.ac.jp/ngo/index.html) is a website for and by NGOs. It was set up as a meeting place for NGOs to discuss work, strategies and results. It is great site to use as a start when looking for information on global NGO movements and activities as well as for reports by and for the UN.

Fund-raising

Actual fund-raising on the internet is still quite small in scale; individuals still have a marked distrust of giving money online. However, we are likely to see more fund-raising taking place in the next few years as e-commerce takes off and distrust declines. Already large charities and non-profits are understanding that the internet offers a valuable and cost-effective way to fund-raise, research, collect donations and grants and keep in touch with funders and potential funders.

Some sites are already accepting online donations, for example ReliefNet (www.reliefnet.org) has been one of the organizations responsible for pioneering an online pledge form. ReliefNet is a non-profit dedicated to helping humanitarian organizations raise global awareness and support for relief efforts via the internet. Instead of accepting money, the site encourages people to pledge money; this is then followed up by a letter and telephone call.

ReliefNet now allows for direct donations. Donors provide their 'First Virtual' account IDs and are charged against their credit cards. Having already provided First Virtual with their credit numbers (usually with a voice telephone call), they merely confirm their donation via e-mail.

Many companies now offer safe ways to give money via the internet. Secure server protocols are perhaps the best known, where credit card details are encrypted during transmission. E-cash is also being introduced, where virtual money can be purchased from trusted companies and then safely spent or donated anywhere on the net.

The Rainforest Action Network (www.ran.org) has a membership and donation form whereby people can donate by telephone or mail, along with an online credit card form which allows donations through the internet.

AlertNet (www.alertnet.org) and CAF provide an easy way for people to give money for emergency relief. AlertNet is funded by the Reuters foundation, the humanitarian arm of the news-gathering group. By using the UK CharityCard, users get the latest news on world emergencies and can pledge money on the

> Virtual money can be purchased from trusted companies and then safely spent or donated anywhere on the net.

net. At the time of writing there are 19 AlertNet charities that accept CharityCard gifts direct, including ActionAid, Afghanaid, CAFOD, Disasters Emergency Committee – Kosovo Appeal Mines Advisory Group, Oxfam, Save the Children Fund and World Vision UK.

Soliciting money from donations is not the only fund-raising option open to NGOs. We shall describe some of the others below.

Banner ads

Fund-raising advertising can be placed on sites free of charge or at a nominal fee. Larger NGOs attracting lots of visitors can also sell banner advertising space on their own sites.

Gifts

In the UK, many non-profit organizations are now offering shopping facilities online. The US Cancer Research Fund offered Valentine cards in 1998. In return for a £5 donation, the cards were e-mailed directly to loved ones. The said loved ones were offered the chance to find out who had sent the card by donating another £5. Cards for Good Causes are a charity Christmas card consortium of 25 member charities, again offering secure purchasing facilities.

Working with corporations and corporate sponsorship

Many of the larger charities in the UK and non-profits in North America have joined forces with commercial organizations to offer services and products. For example, in the UK, British Telecom has funded the Royal British Legion's Global Silence (www.globalsilence.com) website that encourages a two-minute silence at 11a.m. on 11 November to mark the First World War armistice. SurfAid (www.surfaid.org) is a partnership of Christian Aid and internet service provider, Global. Yahoo! has teamed up with both Oxfam and Amnesty International to offer internet access for members and people who want to support their causes. Give On-Line helps individual donors make online donations to NGOs. It provides links and information on charities it supports as well as producing the information and resources to make financial contributions. The donation information is forwarded to non-profits across the USA and the credit card donations are not handled by the site itself but by the non-profit the donor wants it to reach. The site is a *pro bono* service of Data Sense, a Georgia-based company specializing in internet services.

Donations in kind

The Charity Village in Canada is a diverse charity internet site that has created a gifts-in-kind 'flea market' where it costs commercial organizations, or private citizens, $11.00 to host their products per month. In April 1998, the UK organization Shelter (www.shelter.org.uk), with First Direct bank, launched an online appeal based on the idea that net-surfers are 'anoraks'. So why not ask surfers (anoraks) to donate their old anoraks to Shelter in an 'anorak amnesty'?

Online auctions and raffles

Auctions and raffles are extremely popular ways to raise money through the internet. In 1998, Charity Web (www.charityweb.net) was launched to help NGOs raise money by allowing people to pledge items for their favourite charities which would then be sold by auction on the net, with 100% of the sales price going to the charity concerned. Save the Earth held an auction of rock memorabilia in 1996 which featured goods donated by the Rolling Stones and the Red Hot Chilli Peppers. It is believed that this one auction raised over $15,000. ESTOP is a charity auction site for UK charities, including the BBC's Children In Need.

> Two excellent starting points for almost any kind of research are Yahoo! and Infoseek.

Research

Foundations and grant-givers are now getting online and making their grant applications and guidelines available through the internet. Two excellent starting points for almost any kind of research are Yahoo! and Infoseek. An excellent directory to non-profit organizations on the web is Action Without Borders' (www.idealist.org) comprehensive listings. This includes a page on foundations and grant-giving links. Other useful sources include the following:

- **UK Fund-raising** (www.ukfundraising.co.uk) offers help and information on fund-raising with an expertise in online fund-raising for UK charities and non-profits.

- **The UK National Lottery Charities Board** (www.nlcb.org.uk) site includes information on first and second round grant listings, together with current and future grant rounds information.

- **The European Foundation Centre Funders Online Directory** (www.fundersonline.org) offers access to profiles of foundations and corporate funders' websites. The Directory is also searchable by funders' areas of interests.

- **The Grants Centre** (www.waterlooregion.org/cnrn/grants.html) from the Canadian non-profit Resource Network provides a searchable list of grants.

- **Grants-L** (http://tile.net/lists/grantslto.html) is an e-mail discussion list covering funding, grant development requirements and other aspects of developing projects within institutions of higher education around the world.

- **The FundRaiser Cyberzine** (www.fundraiser.com) is a free magazine with news and ideas for fund-raising throughout the world, especially the UK. It is particularly useful for medium-sized groups such as civic groups and small not-for-profit organizations.

- For information on grant giving, visit grantmaker.com/internet.html

5 | Activism

Although we have seen the internet used by political groups, NGOs and the labour movement for some time, it has only been in the past few years that it has really taken off for online activism. Examples range from the Electronic Disturbance Theatre holding virtual sit-ins of Mexican government websites to the occupation of Shell in London in 1998 that involved posting a protest website from the Shell building. Although the company turned the power off and cut the phone lines, the activists involved could still broadcast to people all over the world via the net using simply a digital camera, laptop and a mobile.

Worldwide the web is being used to build online communities to campaign, network and lobby governments. From peaceful and non-violent actions, through environmental protest sites to human rights databases, the net can be used to join campaigns, to research information on corporations and government practices, to apply for funding, hold occupations, publish news the papers will not touch and, more recently, to engage in an entirely new form of activism: electronic civil disobedience or hacktivism.

Direct action has long been a catalyst for social change and just as direct action activists and groups are finding new forms of non-violent protest, so too the web is increasingly being used as the electronic frontier of new protest movements.

And since the internet is often seen as the embodiment of global capitalism many activists argue that it is therefore the best place for the fight. That companies and political parties will pay more attention if protests are made on their own electronic doorsteps.

The internet appears to offer many solutions to old activist problems and it is easy to get carried away, yet activists are now beginning to fully understand what the net can do for activism and where its limitations lie. While the examples of global action have had many positive results, organizing for maximum effectiveness still needs to be done at a local grass-roots level, linking and networking with groups in different countries to share information and pool strategies. The net does not replace the need for physical meetings and direct communication (although some believe the days of physical demonstration and protests are long dead); the majority of activities on the net mimic activism practised in physical reality. This chapter takes a look at some of the most imaginative and innovative uses of the internet by activist groups.

McSpotlight (www.mcspotlight.org) is one of the best known net action websites. Posted on the site you will find a copy of the leaflet 'What's wrong with McDonald's' that sparked the 1997 British libel case against anti-McDonald's campaigners in London. At the time of writing McDonald's have taken no action to have the site closed down, although more people now have access to this leaflet than the original distribution could ever have brought about. We shall return to the McSpotlight site later in this chapter.

Another good example of the more innovative ways in which activists have used the net is in the form of Action Alerts. For example, the Scorecard (www.scorecard.org) site, created by the Environmental Defense Fund (www.edf.org), has created a facility

> Direct action has long been a catalyst for social change.

where, by entering your zip code, you find out what nasty chemicals are in your area. You can then be told who is doing the polluting, what the chemicals are, the effects they have and information on how to contact the polluters to register your protest.

The fightback against globalized capital and the might of transnational and international corporations is very much at home on the internet. Electronic direct action not only supports protests taking place in real time but, in some cases, provides the action itself. For example, Project Underground (www.moles.org) encourages visitors to e-boycott the Shell website because of the company's activities in Nigeria.

We have seen how the net allows geographically dispersed groups and individual campaigners to hook up, share information outside the mainstream media and reduce costs – all making it easier for people to act together. There is an amazing diversity of activists online. At a local level, you will find hundreds of groups from online literacy projects to groups trying to establish local government accountability, recycling schemes, green zones and more cycling routes. There are international Usenet groups such as misc.activism.progressive (http://webmap.missouri.edu/), networks and supersites such as APC and OneWorld. It would appear that while websites are useful in catching attention and spreading the cause to the casual browser, it is e-mail that has the most benefit to activists and campaigners. Closed e-mail lists, discussion and chat allow confidential information to be spread rapidly and cheaply.

Supersites

> Supersites allow for cheap and effective web-hosting.

In theory, the net allows millions of people to have access to your website. In practice, most people won't find you and will never know that you exist. Supersites allow for cheap and effective web-hosting and networking for non-profits, charities and activist groups. By choosing one of these networks, a group immediately enhances its net presence through association with the supersite itself and by becoming more accessible to net-surfers.

OneWorld Online is an amazing site for NGOs and activists of all persuasions. Users include NGO workers, academics, journalists and policy and decision-makers as well as individuals interested in global justice issues and taking action.

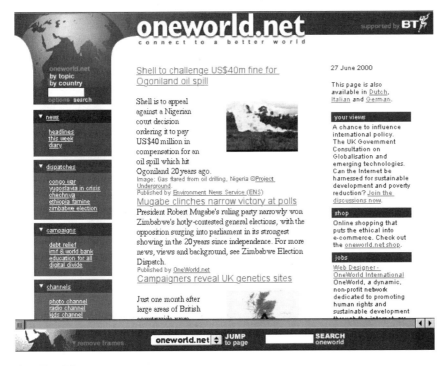

OneWorld

Glen Tarman, publicity manager for OneWorldNet, describes what he sees as the primary focus for OneWorldNet:

OneWorld's mission is to harness the democratic potential of the internet to promote human rights and sustainable development. OneWorld is a global justice communications and networking organization. We use the internet to give people the information they want and need on the most important issues facing humanity in today's world. And through the web we help them to find the organizations they can support to take further action. We are a medium for positive change in the fight for an equitable and just world.

Tarman himself has been been involved in online activism since 1994:

First as a journalist publicizing the opportunities the Internet has for civil society organizations and encouraging them to take it seriously. Then as an individual and in my work for NGOs like VSO [Voluntary Service Overseas] and WDM [World Development Movement] where I co-ordinated national networks of activists across the UK and promoted the work of the organizations online.

What did he see as the advantages of using the internet for activism?

The internet is now the best place to find information on campaigns, issues and strategies for positive change. One of the key advantages is that individuals and organizations with similar concerns can find each other and work together in ways which were not possible in the last decade.

Tarman and OneWorld would list the strengths of using the internet as follows:

1. *Control of message (without distortion by media gatekeepers)*
2. *Cheap (relatively and if in a developed country)*
3. *Constantly accessible 24 hours a day, seven days a week*
4. *Constantly updated and updateable*
5. *Capacity for content is unconstrained*
6. *Chance for innovation*
7. *Cascade effect – distribution of information benefits.*

Tarman continues:

Using the internet for campaigning can be extremely effective. However, never forget that it must be used to complement and supplement other tools, methods and strategies for campaigning. Nothing beats face-to-face communication, networking at meetings IRL [in the real world] and the best organizing tool is often a telephone. Even the campaigns that are acknowledged as deploying the internet with great success such as J18 or the mobilization against the MAI [Multilateral Agreement on Investment] relied on public meetings to organize and communicate. Don't let the internet make you an armchair activist.

Another huge UK site is that of GreenNet (www.gn.apc.org), one of the founding members of the Association for Progressive Communications. GreenNet specializes in networking for environment, peace, human rights and development groups.

GreenNet has provided, among many other things, an international gateway for indigenous networks in Africa and Asia since 1987.

It also offers training and support to members, and a newsletter, *AlterNet News*, which carries brief news items, campaign updates, a diary of key forthcoming events and announcements as well as information on GreenNet, the activities of its member organizations and community.

GreenNet itself started in 1986 and in 1989 began collaborating with similar networks in other countries. It was from this collaboration that the APC was formed in 1990.

GreenNet is part of the only global computer network specifically designed for environment, peace, human rights and development groups. It offers email and its own special conferences, as well as the usual range of dial-up Internet services. The interface is designed to be easy and quick to use for those who don't know much about computers. Staff have extensive experience with, and contacts in, political/social movements, coupled with expertise in information technology and its applications.

GreenNet Headlines, 26th June 2000:

- 'Elections are not the same thing as democracy'. Parliamentary elections took place in Zimbabwe at the weekend (June 24th and 25th). Click here for more news, comment and links from Zimbabwe.

- Amnesty International have written an open letter to members of the House of Lords expressing their concerns over the lack of safeguards against human rights violations

ABOUT GN ■

ACTIVITIES ■

RESOURCES ■

SUPPORT ■

SERVICES ■

SEARCH ■

CONTACT ■

We are pleased to announce a new service - searchable archives of the InterPress News Agency.

Over 300 members have web sites on GreenNet, click here for the members directory.

AlterNet, fortnightly Civil Society e-zine.

The international charitable work of GreenNet Limited is implemented through the GreenNet Educational Trust (GET).

GreenNet is a founding member of the Association for Progressive Communications.

built into the RIP Bill. The Bill is in Committee stage in the House of Lords on 28th June.

- 'A stark warning to others' or 'a tragedy waiting to happen'? Britain's asylum policies are called into question after 58 people died in a sealed lorry while trying to enter this country. Several meetings have been called in support of asylum seekers.

GreenNet

The APC could be described as a global network of networks. By sharing information and technology they showed there was not only a need for an international host and server site for peace, human rights and environmental groups but that such a site could work and continue to exist. Their work can roughly be said to include the following:

■ *Advocacy and facilitation*. Assisting NGOs and civil society movements through use of information and communications technology.

■ *Internet rights*. Alerting and campaigning in the defence of internet rights and space for NGOs.

■ *Network development*. Building the capacity of members and new members for communication.

■ *Working with members*. For example, the APC Women's Networking Support Programme promotes gender-aware development, and African members' programmes strengthen indigenous information-sharing and independent networking capacity.

Another excellent example of an internet activism supersite is EnviroLink (www.envirolink.org). This site hosts and provides links to hundreds of direct action, environmental and animal rights websites in the UK, Europe and North America.

www.tao.ca is a Canadian supersite and server established in 1996, which helps to facilitate communication, research and organizing for TAO members, TAO being an acronym for The Anarchy Organization. The site runs on the Linux operating system, providing e-mail, e-mail lists and web hosting to members. It is broken down into Tao symbol areas, with, for example, the Sky section containing information on the TAO organization itself, while the Earth section is concerned with human liberation and popular revolution. The Wind section deals with communication, networks and shared struggles and how to get involved in the different currents mentioned.

One of the biggest and best sites for news on real-time and internet-based direct action is Protest net (www.protest.net). This site provides a brilliant directory of actions taking place across the world, direct links to the groups undertaking campaigns and ways for you to get involved – either by use of the internet or by turning up to a meeting or real-life protest.

New types of activism

The Worldwide Fund for Nature (www.panda.org) has really thought about how to develop its online campaigning. They have set up the Conservation Action Network. This is an electronic advocacy network that lets you help save wildlife and wild spaces without moving from your computer. So far, participants in the network have helped protect the Galapagos Islands, the Everglades, sea turtles, tigers and rhinos. WWF have created a Personal Action centre for members, which includes information on taking action, sends out e-mails and action alerts and gives the user the know-how to modify and change their centre to suit their own needs.

Other sites use 'cultural jamming' techniques – taking the messages of corporate society and turning them around to a form of resistance. Culturejam.com records and promotes anti-commercial information from independent videos and audio recordings, while the Billboard Liberation Front (www.billboardliberationfront.com) tells you to how modify, enhance and liberate roadside signs. Adbusters (www.adbusters.org/) is a global network of artists, writers, students and educators who seek to use the net to create social activism. The Adbusters magazine, also available from their site, has some very innovative and imaginative anti-ads to look at, as well as links to other culture jamming sites.

Blissett is a 'collective avatar' which allows individuals to act both on and off the net using the identity of Luther Blissett. Luther Blissett (www.lutherblissett.net) came into existence in Italy and refers to the UK footballer of the same name. Former Watford, AC Milan and England player Luther Blissett is rather bemused at becoming a figurehead for direct action groups and anarchists on the web. It all started with young anarchists in Rome who, when stopped for not having tickets to travel on trains, gave their names as 'Luther Blissett'. At court, they continued to insist they were all Luther Blissett. Blissett's name may have been used in retaliation against right-wing groups who objected to black footballers in Italy.

> Conservation Action Network lets you help save wildlife and wild spaces without moving from your computer.

News of the Luther Blissett Project was published in the magazine *Derive Approdi* in March 1995. Blissett has since become famous, or at least notorious, for media terrorism actions such as false news about non-existent satanic cults, and has even authored some books.

Act Up (www.actupny.org/) is a site for information and campaigning on AIDS and gay liberation. Their website supports the direct action they take in the real world and includes streaming video.

Act Up, which is well known for AIDS awareness campaigns directed at government inaction and drug company profiteering, is generally credited with reviving civil disobedience tactics in the USA. On the site you will find a 30-minute online training video which explains how and why activists use civil disobedience, as well as electronic guidelines for direct actions and on how to practice non-violence. It includes a good clear information area on legal issues (including what to do if arrested) and a page about and for jail solidarity. The streaming video netcast, at the time of writing, was temporarily out of action.

The US-based Right-to-Know Network (RTK Net at www.rtk.net) is a powerful example of how the internet can be a useful tool for community-based activists. RTK Net is an easy-to-use online database that contains a wealth of information about pollution and waste within communities.

The site provides online copies of the numerous reports that industries and businesses are required to file with various federal agencies, including inventories of toxic chemicals and incident reports on toxic spills. This information is searchable by address as well as by company name, and information is available in both detailed and summary form.

The Ruckus Society (www.ruckus.org) is a US NGO set up in 1995 to train activists in non-violent forms of resistance, its website giving information on activist skills and its activist camps as well as up-to-date information on activism around the world. The site was instrumental in providing both information and training for US-based activism with the Carnival against Capitalism and the World Trade Organization (WTO) Seattle actions.

Disabled People's Direct Action Network (www.disabilitynet.co.uk) is an incredibly good example of how an activist site can look if some thought is put into it. This is a British site which focuses on British issues but much of the content is useful to the international movement. You can learn a lot about direct action and campaign-organizing by visiting this site.

The Free Burma Coalition (www.freeburma.org), which aims to persuade investors to get out of Myanmar (previously called Burma), set up a website in September 1995. The internet campaign facilitated by this site in 1997 was instrumental in PepsiCo's decision to withdraw from Myanmar. Texaco and Heineken are among others persuaded not to invest in, or buy from, the country. Visit their website to find out how they did it.

Automated Activism (www.we-2.com/popc/organic_link.html) is a service provided by Pop Conscious (and yes, they may try and sell you a few CDs in the process). The site states that it can simplify the process of having a say in public affairs by allowing you to send a pre-written e-mail message to a list of important politicians and policy-makers expressing your concerns. At the time of writing you could click on the following to e-mail letters: End Corporate Monopoly of Public Airwaves; Goodbye organic food, hello sewer sludge; and Navy Sonar Threatens Marine Life.

The Tactical Media Crew (www.tmcrew.org/) and Network have various mechanisms on their site which help you to become an electronic activist by the click of a mouse. In November 1999, the site highlighted the encryption legislation issues in the USA with their International Arms Trafficker Training Page. This takes the form of a web page providing a three-line encryption program. It is a protest against the US International Traffic in Arms Regulations (ITAR) which classify encryption as exporting munitions. The site says

---

Clicking the submit button below is an act of civil disobedience, and will make you an International Arms Trafficker.

Optional Info on Munitions Exporter (this means you):

1. Name:

2. E-mail Address:

3. How public do you want your protest to be?

 Don't tell anyone that I'm an arms trafficker

 Add me to the public list of Known Arms Traffickers

 Add me to the list and send a letter to the president for me

---

Along with the name and address you enter, your current host name and IP address are added to the list or the e-mail, if you decide to be that public. Sending e-mail may take 20 seconds or more, but it is worth it, since you get a 'thank you note' from the president.

Boycotts

Electronic boycotts are among the new tools of net activism. A boycott is a way of responding to a given situation where a company or government is acting in a way which is unacceptable to consumers, organizations or individuals who will suffer due to their actions. The Boycott Board (www.2street.com/boycott) provides socially-minded consumers with the information and means to take a stance against exploitative companies throughout the world. The Boycott Board acts as a bulletin board where groups can post entries in a database which is then available to surfers. The Boycott Nike site (www.saigon.com/nike) urges visitors to write to Nike protesting at their employment practices in South East Asia.

Boycott Shell Gas On The Information Highway was a good example of how electronic boycotts can work. Activists can also subscribe to an e-mail discussion list that focuses on the Shell campaign. To subscribe to Shell-Nigeria-action, send e-mail to listproc@essential.org with the message: 'subscribe shell-nigeria-action your-e-mail-address' in the message.

Consumer issues

Clean Clothes Campaign (www.cleanclothes.org/) lists urgent online appeals, from petitions to e-mail letters. Sweatshop Watch (www.sweatshopwatch.org) is a coalition of labour, community, civil rights, immigrant rights, women's and religious organizations, and individuals committed to eliminating sweatshop conditions in the garment industry. The Just Shoppers' Guide, although geared to a New Zealand audience, provides comprehensive information on practices to do with ethical shopping which would apply anywhere in the northern hemisphere. For example,

> Electronic boycotts are among the new tools of net activism.

information is provided on the Nestlé boycott. There is also information on Buy Nothing Day (www.adbusters.org/campaigns/bnd), which also has its own website.

Other boycott sites

Boycott of dictator states: www.geocities.com/CapitolHill/8929/gb.html
Boycott Nike: www.saigon.com/~nike/

Online petitions

Online petitions enable people to demonstrate support or opposition by signing an e-mail or website-based petition. These electronic petitions are an increasingly popular way to organize people into action. There are many drawbacks however, and caution

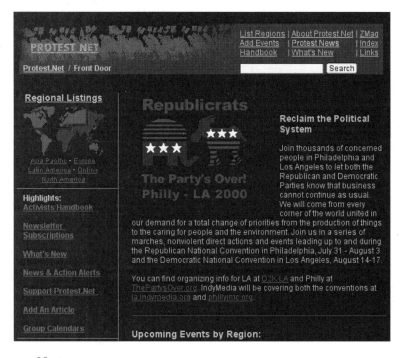

Protest.Net

should be used. Petitions tend to hang around the electronic ether for a long time and many organizations have neglected to put an end date on their petitions, with responses still arriving years later.

Recently SchNews (www.schNews.org.uk), a Brighton-based direct action group in the UK, were involved in setting up a petition to protest against new legislation on terrorism. A brilliant website was set up explaining why, by supporting Nelson Mandela before the end of apartheid for example, you would now fall foul of proposed UK anti-terrorist legislation. It then invited people to tick a series of boxes each giving a reason for 'why I am a terrorist'. This is then e-mailed anonymously or with the person's own e-mail address to Jack Straw, the British Home Secretary, along with media outlets including Red Pepper (www.redpepper.org.uk). We at Red Pepper can personally testify to the traffic this must have generated, as being on the cc list meant we received every single e-mail sent to Jack Straw. We were kindly taken off this list (our old equipment simply could not cope) but not before having received over 500 e-mails in a few days. This is an extremely effective way to engage people in e-activism and a very good example of how with a little imagination activists can respond to legislation or abuse quickly and effectively.

The EnviroLink (www.envirolink.org) site provides many examples of online petitions. As of November 1999, these included petitions against cruelty to bears in China, a petition to stop pet ownership of primates, an anti-bullfighting petition, a petition against the control of animals in São Paulo through mass culling and a petition to secure the mandatory labelling of all genetically- engineered foods.

One site, E-The People (www.e-thepeople.com), has hundreds of petitions to choose from, and 170,000 e-mail addresses of government officials.

Another good example of online petitions is the Abolition 2000 International Petition. Abolition 2000 (www.abolition2000.org) is a global network comprising more than 1350 citizen action groups in 88 countries. More than 13 million individual signatures have been collected for the petition, outlined below.

Missiles to Sunflowers: A New Commitment for a New Century

We call upon all states, and particularly the nuclear weapons states, to make the following commitments:

1. END THE NUCLEAR THREAT. End the nuclear threat by de-alerting all nuclear weapons, withdrawing all nuclear weapons from foreign soil and international waters, separating warheads from delivery vehicles and disabling them, committing to unconditional no first use of nuclear weapons, and ceasing all nuclear weapons tests, including laboratory tests and 'subcriticals.'

2. SIGN THE TREATY. Sign a Nuclear Weapons Convention by the year 2000, agreeing to the elimination of all nuclear weapons within a timebound framework.

3. REALLOCATE RESOURCES. Reallocate resources to ensure a sustainable global future and to redress the environmental devastation and human suffering caused by nuclear weapons production and testing, which have been disproportionately borne by the world's indigenous peoples.

Start a signature campaign today. Print out a hard copy of the petition I want to sign the e.mail version of the International Petition

Signer's First Name:

Signer's Last Name:

Address:

City:

State/Province:

Zip Code:

Country:

Phone:

E-mail:*

Electronic civil disobedience

The old tactics of civil disobedience are increasingly being adopted on the internet.

Most of the resistance on the net confines itself either to offering alternative information services or to organizing around issues of autonomy such as free speech. However, as activists become increasingly sophisticated in their use of electronic communications, the old tactics of civil disobedience are increasingly being adopted on the internet: from virtual sit-ins to e-mail blockage of government and corporate computers causing shut-down or suspension of operations. Internet warfare theorists argue that, in today's information society, nations and corporations are increasingly vulnerable to information-based attacks.

In 1994 the Critical Art Ensemble (www.critical-art.net/) produced an electronic essay entitled *Electronic Disturbance* in which they argue that as capitalism has become increasingly mobile, dispersed and electronic so resistance needs to take the same form. They reason that to confront capital, resistance must be strongest in the places capital is now strongest – the internet. However, they believe the net should be only one arm of civil disobedience which needs to be utilized and combined with direct action on the streets.

The Electronic Disturbance Theatre (EDT) (www.thing.net/~rdom/ecd/ecd.html) are described as cyber activists who are developing the theory and practice of electronic civil disobedience (ECD). Up to now their focus has been mainly on the Mexican and US governments.

EDT has created an internet program called FloodNet (www.thing.net/~rdom/ecd/ecd.html) which is URL-based software used to flood and block an opponent's website. Clicking on the applet image (which contains a representation of the targeted site) sends a predefined message to the server error log. Alternatively, surfers may voice their political concerns on a targeted server via the 'personal message' form which sends the surfer's own statement to the server error log.

To use FloodNet, surfers follow a link and then simply leave their browser open. The intent is to disrupt access to the targeted website by flooding the host server with requests for that page.

Criticism of these tactics has come from other organizations involved in the Zapatistas support movement. The actions have been called 'reckless' and the EDT described as being more concerned about hype than the causes they say they are engaged in. Some believe this kind of disruption will brand the Zapatistas as 'enemies of freedom and communication', allowing the Mexican government to step up its own underhand activities against the Zapatistas both in cyberspace and the off-line world.

Electronic sit-ins

An example of a call for an electronic sit-in follows.

'Tuesday, 23-Nov-1999 13:56:11 EST

A – I n f o s a multi-lingual news service by, for, and about anarchists

'VIRTUAL SIT-IN' AT A LEADING WEBSITE PLANNED TO COINCIDE WITH THE WTO's SEATTLE CONFERENCE

For details of how to take part visit the NEW 'electrohippies' website at:

http://www.gn.apc.org/pmhp/ehippies/

TARGET WILL BE REVEALED AT 00.01GMT, 30/11/99

A new website has started up to promote 'virtual activism' in the UK and Europe. The site is all about taking action, and undertaking civil Disobedience, using the core of modern society – its electronic information and communications infrastructure. Why? Because technology enables a lot of the destruction that takes place in the world, but like most technology it is not innately bad – it's just the people who are in charge of it. Technology also allows people to have anonymity because their communications and planning are kept remote from the public arena.

What we're out to do is change all that by extending the philosophy of activism and direct action into the 'virtual' world of electronic information exchange and communications. Of course, in the scale of things we can't hope to be more effecting than an annoying mosquito. But we can let them know that they can't use technology as a veil to obscure the public's concern about the future of the planet.

IN SUPPORT OF THE GLOBAL ACTION TO MARK THE WORLD TRADE ORGANIZATION'S SEATTLE CONFERENCE, WE WILL BE PROVIDING AN OPPORTUNITY FOR PEOPLE TO TAKE PART IN AN ON-LINE 'VIRTUAL SIT-IN'.

At midnight, Greenwich Mean Time, on the 30th November, the 'action page' will be loaded with information on how you can register your protest against the WTO's Seattle conference. The page will operate for seven days.

We hope that during this period you will access this page as often as possible and take part in the sit-in. There will be precise details posted on November 30th. There will also be files to download in order to set up mirror-sites on your own server in order to spread the capacity of the sit-in. If you would like to receive the files direct by e-mail on November the 30th, along with all the information on how to run the sit-in from where ever you are in the world, then send a request to ehippies@tesco.net.

We hope that you enjoy participating in this event.

Once again, the address of the site is:

http://www.gn.apc.org/pmhp/ehippies/

END

from the electrohippies – ehippies@tesco.net

Land, ecology and genetics

> Environmental groups retain a very high presence on the web.

Environmental groups retain a very high presence on the web and surveys have revealed that of all causes in which surfers have expressed interest the environment is the leader.

The UK, Leeds Earth First is part of the bigger coalition of Earth First (www.htrc.ac.uk/campaigns/earthfirst.html). The Leeds site is very well organized, with some good links as well as information on their campaigns. The site explains how to get involved in actions, and provides resources for students and journalists. You can even download the Earth First font. Their E-mail Action update will give you information on ecological actions throughout the UK, the newsletter being passed to different groups each year and written by activists for networking and publishing campaigns.

The Land is Ours (TLIO) (www.oneworld.org/tlio/index.html) is a UK-based direct action and campaigning group. The site is hosted by OneWorld and EnviroLink. It gives details on current campaigns, actions and news as well as information on local groups, land right groups and meetings of TLIO. There are also details of books, pamphlets and newsletters.

The carnival against capitalism

On 18 June 1999 (J18), hundreds of thousands of activists protested against global capitalism. Environmentalists, workers, the unemployed, indigenous peoples, trade unionists, peasant groups, women's networks, the landless, students and peace activists throughout the world gathered in a global protest to coincide with the first day of the G8 (Group of Eight richest nations) summit in Kola, Germany.

Much has been made of the use of the internet in the organization of J18. There were hundreds of websites involved in organizing across the world and a J18 e-mail list.

In the UK, Justice and Reclaim the Streets (RTS) (www.gn.apc.org/rts/) used the internet to aid their day of action. The RTS site includes information on the action taken across the world and specifically in the UK together with articles and information on the follow-up to the day. Their site gives links to and reports on people who had been jailed around the world for their part in demonstrations and actions, some sites providing links so you can e-mail support. The RTS website gives an update diary; there is an archive, essays and literature explaining how RTS is a 'disorganization' which may include you.

The Bay Area, New York City and Toronto RTSs all have pictures and information on J18 and what happened in their respective areas. The J18 site, hosted by GreenNet, has mirrors throughout the world and is available in Castellano, German, English, Russian, Dutch, Italian and French. Much new information on the site is rebuttal of the press coverage that J18 brought about.

Pirate TV helped provide live webcasts throughout the day to 43 countries around the world. There was a chatroom up and running which allowed people to discuss and report events. In

Melbourne and Sydney sites were set up that carried out live webcasting on actions.

In J18, the internet became a battleground between activists and the corporate world, with companies in the affected cities passing e-mails back and forth on the status of the protest and the measures they were taking to protect themselves.

The McSpotlight site

The McSpotlight site, run by supporters of the 'McLibel Two', went online in February 1996. It is run by volunteers in 22 countries, with mirror sites in four countries. It contains 20,000 files – most relating to McDonald's and the trial – and claims more than a million visitors a month. In a Beyond McD's section, it targets other corporations and focuses on their business practices. These include Pfizer, Johnson & Johnson, Boots the Chemist, Philip Morris, BAT, Nestlé, Cow & Gate, Milupa,

McSpotlight

Unilever, Proctor & Gamble, SmithKline Beecham, Colgate-Palmolive and Shell.

The site gives a Guided Tour of the McDonald's own website, presenting the actual site within its own frames and giving a critical commentary.

The McSpotlight site started in response to the McDonald's libel action against Helen Steel and Dave Morris (the 'McLibel Two') who had distributed leaflets entitled *What's wrong with McDonald's*. Thus began the longest libel trial in the UK. The website gives official court transcripts, including witness statements. It is well designed with good navigation tools, and its mirror sites enable you to get fast access to the site nearest to you. Some of the ways in which it exhorts people to help include volunteering for the campaign, donating money, giving a wish-list of what's needed for the campaign, a global forum for debating McDonald's, an Adopt a Store section where you can help leaflet UK McDonald's and a McSpotlight Kit to download a compressed version of the site which helps to ensure McDonald's cannot stop the dissemination of information about the company. In detail:

■ 'Anti-McDonald's Pledge: add your name to the thousands pledging to continue distributing anti-McDonald's information whatever the verdict in the McLibel trial.

■ Leaflets: print off and circulate the *What's wrong with McDonald's* leaflets (available in at least 12 languages), and other similar leaflets.

■ McSpotlight mailing list: subscribe to this mailing list to keep up to date with all the McSpotlight news and events.

■ McLibel list server: subscribe to this mailing list to receive regular updates of the McLibel case and the anti-McDonald's campaign.

■ The Debating Room: join in the global debate about McDonald's and all the company stands for in McSpotlight's own moderated discussion group.

■ Donations: make a donation to the McLibel case, to McSpotlight or to the McLibel documentary.

Corporate Watch

Corporate Watch (www.corporatewatch.org) is an online magazine and resource centre that not only investigates corporate practices but also supplies tools to help activists do the same.

Corporate Watch was born on the internet as one of the first groups to recognize the role of technology in and for activism. The site is wonderfully designed. Every year the Greenwash Award is given to the company that Corporate Watch believes has done the most in terms of public relations (PR) to promote itself as a green or ecologically sound company whilst allegedly at the same time not following such practices. The term 'greenwash' is now included in the *Concise Oxford Dictionary* and is defined as 'Disinformation disseminated by an organization so as to present an environmentally responsible public image. Derivatives greenwashing (n). Origin from green on the pattern of whitewash'.

The Multinationals Resource Center (MRC) (www.essential.org/monitor/monitor.html) is a project of *Multinational Monitor* magazine. MRC is designed to help activists, journalists, academics and others who need information on the activities of corporations operating in their communities.

Other good links

Corporate governance: www.corpgove.net/
Ending corporate governance: www.ratical.com/corporations/
The Octopus: http://burn.uscd.edu/~mai.octopus.html
Global Trade Watch: www.citizen.org/pctrade/tradehome.html

Corporations fight back

'Astroturf' and 'greenwashing' are terms used to indicate 'manufactured' public protest by corporate PR interests, and are increasingly used by corporations on the web. For example, Reebok have set up awards for Human Rights and naturally have a web page dedicated to this, to show their corporate responsibilities as caring, sharing and really quite nice people. The Reebok Human Rights Awards Page contains brief biographies and photographs of human rights activists all over the world.

Reebok International is not the only corporation to be putting forward a message of caring and concern both in real time and through the internet. The Royal Dutch Shell site includes platforms where critics can vent their opinions. A large part of the Shell website gives information on company ethics and attempts to counter activists and critics by creating a forum section for debate on ethical issues as well as supplying links to Greenpeace (www.greenpeace.org) and Friends of the Earth. The current Shell website receives about 1000 e-mail messages a month, and a full-time staff member personally responds to all of them within 48 hours. All this may seem jolly good stuff until you remember that the image portrayed by the site might not be one shared by the Ogoni peoples. Both McDonald's and Nike (www.nikebiz.com) dedicate parts of their websites to messages on environmental and labour practices. This is also leading to the emergence of new internet companies such as eWatch in the USA that trace discussions taking place about major corporations on the web and report back on how to spin more appropriate messages.

Resources for activists

The Public Register's Annual Report Service (www.prars.com)
Allows you to search for a corporate annual report. The Web100 gives the websites of the 100 largest US and global corporations. Use Paydirt Online Search (www.paydirtonline.com) for oil, gas and mining corporations.

Greenpeace CyberActivist (www.suncore.org/ contents_take_action.html) Greenpeace has a CyberActivist section where you can volunteer to take part in internet actions as part of their cyber activist team; a recent way was by sending e-mails to the European Union (EU) commissioners for health and consumer protection urging a ban on all soft PVC toys for under-threes in Europe.

The Official Mad Cow Disease Home Page (www.mad-cow.org)
This takes a look at BSE and has humorous visuals on the symptoms to look for. It has good links and an archive with about 5100 articles on BSE and CJD plus news on cows being fed human sewage, how BSE tests have been ignored and how oxblood can be found in red wine. The Mad Scientist section gives links to information on who is working in this field and where information has been censored. It is part of the CJD web-ring.

Environmental Defense Fund (www.edf.org) A predominantly US site, but with much global application. In addition to using alerts and news, it encourages site visitors to join the EDF Activist Network. You can fill in a form online and commit to taking at least three actions in a 12-month period; these actions are e-mailed to you once you have joined. The site also hosts forums and has a list of practical actions to help the environment such as a guide to greener paper and green electricity.

The Clearinghouse on Environmental Research and Advocacy (CLEAR) (www.ewg.org/pub/home/clear/clear.html) A Washington DC group that monitors and reports on the anti-environmental 'wise use' movement. Wise use refers to organizations and corporations that are attempting to roll back or weaken laws that protect wildlife and health and safety standards for water, food and air by producing and distributing information to counter the research done on the impact to our health and that of the planet by these very companies. They will often distort statistics and information to this end.

Rainforest Action Network (www.ran.org) A well-designed website which includes action alerts that allow you send your messages on saving the rainforests to environmental protection agencies directly from the site. It also gives information on boycott campaigns, resources for teachers and an online quiz to test your knowledge of the rainforests.

Amnesty International The Amnesty International/International Secretariat site (www.amnesty.org/) contains a wealth of information, searchable databases, online reports, press releases and other material.

The East Timor Action Network (www.etan.org) Provides information about and ways to help East Timor. The group advocates changing US foreign policy and urges support for self-determination and upholding of human rights in East Timor, which was invaded by Indonesia in 1975.

Derechos Café (www.derechos.net/) A clearing house of net human rights resources with a focus on Latin America. Also features Action In Solidarity with Indonesia and East Timor National Coalition to Abolish the Death Penalty.

> The Amnesty International site contains a wealth of information.

Human Rights Watch (www.hrw.org) Founded in 1978 as Helsinki Watch, this is a coalition of independent human rights groups. The site contains information about Human Rights Watch itself and has extensive information about human rights conditions sorted by country and region.

The File Room (www.thefileroom.org) Records censored works and gives information about censorship through history.

Gay and Lesbian Alliance Against Defamation (www.glaa.org) News updates, action items and an Alertline to report homophobia. Also includes the GLAD Scoreboard, which tracks the number of gay and lesbian characters on television sitcoms.

National Gay and Lesbian Task Force (www.ngltf.org/) A good and informative US site with lots of news updates, good links to other sites and even a job bank.

Voices in the Wilderness (www.nonviolence.org/vitw) VIW is an international loose group of activists who have taken action against the Iraqi sanctions. They believe it is a moral imperative to break the sanctions in order to help the children and the sick who are dying simply because of the lack of basic medical supplies. The site illustrates why the VIW takes action, and includes an illustration of the current meagre contents of an Iraqi food ration basket. One of their actions was a week-long vigil during which people were asked to eat only the contents of such a basket. The website has downloadable educational material that gives details on how you can help, from organizing delegations and vigils to writing to newspapers.

School of the Americas Watch (www.soaw.org) The US Army School of the Americas, Georgia, trains Latin American soldiers in combat, counter-insurgency, and counter-narcotics. Graduates have been responsible for some of the worst human rights abuses in Latin America. They include Manuel Noriega of Panama, Leopoldo Galtieri and Roberto Viola of Argentina, Juan Velasco Alvarado of Peru, Guillermo Rodriguez from Ecuador, and Hugo Banzer Suarez of Bolivia. SOA Watch seeks to close the US Army School of the Americas through vigils and fasts, demonstrations and non-violent protest. The website is informative and well designed with pages on graduates of the schools, their manuals, previous protests, a good FAQ sheet and an SOA Watch newsletter. There is also a non-violence training handbook, details of local vigils and events and songs on the 'Sing it Down: Songs to Close the SOA page'.

PeaceNet (www.peacenet.apc.org/peacenet) The first and largest international computer network for activists in peace, human rights and related issues. The site contains information about a number of human rights, peace, environment and other 'progressive' issues.

International Peace Bureau (IPB) (www.ipb.org) Based in Geneva and founded in 1892, their website provides links to their partner organizations including their favourite sites. The IPB is the world's oldest and most comprehensive international peace federation, bringing people together. The site contains press information initiatives, information on programmes and conferences, ways to help the project and a peace calendar.

> The IPB is the world's oldest and most comprehensive international peace federation.

Nuclear News on the Web (www.wagingpeace.org/news/ nukenews.html) Includes an online newsletter, calendar, action alerts and articles. Their mailing lists and newsletters are extensive and include *Arms Control Today*. NukeNet is a list server (or e-mail mailing list) for the distribution of news, fact sheets and action alerts regarding nuclear issues, predominantly nuclear power and nuclear waste.

The Nonviolence Web (www.nonviolence.org) Has an information discussion group and hosts a wide range of peace organizations such as Fellowship of Reconciliation, an interfaith movement committed to creating peace and justice. The Nuclear Resister provides information on arrest for anti-nuclear civil resistance in the USA and Canada. The International Service for Peace (SIPAZ) is a non-violent, grass-roots coalition of peace groups working in Chiapas as human rights observers.

The Big, Big List of Nuclear Related Links (www.fas.org/ nuke/hew/) A comprehensive and on the whole working list of links to topics on peace and disarmament. The links cover various areas including activism, arms control, historical documentation and references, the military and world governments, and weapons of mass distruction.

ProActivist.com This site is dedicated to photographically documenting protests and demonstrations. It has a good index of links, a bulletin board and, for the lonely among you, progressive personals.

United Nations High Commissioner for Refugees (www.unhcr.ch) The official homepage for the UNHCR. Contains refugee and nationality legislation from over 100 countries, a huge number of international conventions, such as the Rights of the Child, and so on.

DIANA Human Rights Database (www.law.us.edu/Diana/) A project of the Urban Morgan Human Rights Institute at the University of Cincinnati College of Law, this gives text versions of all international human rights instruments and extensive bibliographies on human rights.

The Electronic Democracy Information Network Gopher (www.hrweb.org/resource.html) Links to an enormous number of United Nations, United States and NGO human rights documents.

Norbert's Bookmarks for Active People (www.dfg-vk.de/english/book02.htm) Over 1000 links dedicated to the following topics: peace, non-violence, disarmament, human rights, environment, third world social issues and politics.

ASEED Europe (Action for Solidarity, Equality, Environment and Development) (www.antenna.nl/aseed/) A European network of youth groups campaigning on environment and development issues like the World Bank and the International Monetary Fund (IMF), climate and multinationals.

Bellona (www.bellona.no/e/bellona/) An eastern European site with industrial pollution nuclear issues (mainly waste and reprocessing) in Russia, the Baltic states and Finland.

Universal Black Pages (www.ubp.com) Organizes the information available on the internet about black history, music, colleges and culture.

Anti-Defamation League (ADL) (www.adl.org) ADL has a Hate Filter that will block hate sites in order to help parents prevent children from inadvertently stepping into racist sites. The software can be downloaded from the website.

HateWatch (www.hatewatch.org) A Cambridge-based organization monitoring hate material on the web, this is not only to do with racial hatred but also bigotry and violence against other minority groups such as lesbians and gay men. HateWatch.org has created a catalogue of about 400 organizational-based hate sites, bulletin boards and e-mail lists.

Artists Against Racism (AAR) (www.artistsagainstracism.com) Educates youth worldwide though campaigns to promote tolerance and equality.

Further resources

Peace and anti-war issues

The Centre for War and Peace Studies: www.cwps.org
CovertAction Quarterly: www.caq.com
For mother earth: www.motherearth.org
Epeace – send to world leaders: www.epeace.com
Disarmament links: www.igc.apc.org
Nobel Peace Prize Internet Archives: www.almaz.com/nobel/peace
War Resisters International: www.netaxs.com/~nvweb/wrl/
Conscientious objectors: www.objector.org
Peace News: www.gn.apc.org/peacenews/
Peacewire: www.peacewire.org
United Nations gopher: gopher://gopher.undp.org

Race issues

African American holocaust: www.maafa.org
Black history database: www.ai.mit.edu/~isbell/HFh/black/
Affirmative action and diversity page: http://aad.english.ucsb.edu/
Anti-racism resources: www.pleiades-net.com/choice/web/TARRHP.1.
html
Coalition for human rights of immigrants: http://home.earthlink.
net/~dbwilson/chri/
Black Information Network: www.bin.com
Malcolm X: a research site: www.brothermalcom.net
Martin Luther King: www.thekingcenter.com
Multiracial Activist: www.multiracial.com

6

The Developing World and the Internet

Unless African countries become full actors in the global information revolution, the gap between the haves and have-nots will widen, opening the possibility to increased marginalisation of the continent The gap will increase the likelihood of cultural, religious and tribal ghettos leading to regional and inter-regional conflicts.

PARTICIPANT AT SYMPOSIUM ON *TELEMATICS FOR DEVELOPMENT IN AFRICA*, ADDIS ABABA, APRIL 1995

In 1997 the ITU/BDT (International Telecommunications Union/ Telecommunication Development Bureau) Telecommunication Indicator database documented that half the global population had never used a telephone, let alone could imagine what the internet looked like or meant.

Exclusion from the internet means exclusion from information, which then contributes to maintaining the current unequal and injust balance of power between North and South. As we move towards an information age, many developing countries risk exclusion, lacking the infrastructure and resources to make the internet a readily available part of their society. For many countries access restrictions mean they are on the slow lane on the Information Superhighway.

In many parts of the developing world internet access is not only restricted by lack of telecommunication infrastructure and poor financial resources but also because of literacy levels. In India and Africa, for example, literacy rates are still poor and only small percentages of the educated portion of the population are able to use the net. This, in turn, can precipitate a 'brain drain' as lack of access to electronic libraries and e-mail facilities means many technology experts and academics who cannot hope to keep up to date with developments in their field are tempted to emigrate.

In some countries the value of the internet and telecommunication is creating a double standard system. Governments want to develop technology and attract new, and predominantly western, business to their countries whilst restricting access to their own citizens.

The building of capable and cheap electronic networks is still a major consideration and one that needs to be addressed urgently. The African continent is still highly dependent on third-party networks, usually in the USA. At present direct access to the internet is restricted to about 40 countries, including Zimbabwe, Ghana, Zambia, Mozambique, Egypt and South Africa. IT development is not cheap and is in competition with more short-term urgent needs such as healthcare and famine relief. However, connectivity may help in the long run with many of these problems; for example, better healthcare information via the internet to geographically dispersed and inaccessible regions may benefit the peoples of these areas enormously. The availability of information on the net, from websites to interactive discussion forums, can help people communicate across the world; African researchers and academics can link up with counterparts in Europe to discuss relevant issues, as can agriculturists and farmers to find information on topics from climate control to genetically modified foods.

The internet also has many advantages for developing countries in education, for example, distance learning. Books and magazines are extremely expensive in Africa, costs of production, storage and transport often putting them out of reach for ordinary Africans and even libraries. The internet can make publications available online far more cheaply, via CD-ROMs, websites and e-mail. And the 'instant response' offered by e-mail can be instrumental in human rights and development issues, as we shall now see.

Comparative research on wages carried out on the internet, and e-mail lobbying of western activists and trade unionists, has helped Guatemalan workers gain wage increases from PepsiCo Inc.

> Exclusion from the internet means exclusion from information.

In 1998 e-mail was used extensively by Indonesian women's movements protesting against human rights abuses. The Perempuan (women) e-group list provided a clearing house tool for the women's organizations that emerged after the resignation of Suharto, including the Indonesian women's coalition for justice and democracy. This group used e-mail to provide a cheap and quick way to circulate information and gain feedback on women's rights in Jakarta and throughout the Indonesian archipelago. The e-mail messages that reached the rest of the world caused a flood of protests.

A supersite that we mentioned in Chapter 5, OneWorldNet, works in partnership with the South. Publicity manager Glen Tarman explains,

> *OneWorld is a partnership organization. Around a fifth of our hundreds of NGO partners are based in the South and we aim to increase this proportion. We promote their website content through the high visibility editorial sections of our portal as well as indexing their sites so their material is available through the OneWorld search engine. We take their message and stories to our global audience. In addition, we also provide capacity-building training on using the internet through our offices in Africa and South Asia.*

> *Our next phase of increasing Southern voices on the internet will be new specialist supersites on global issues. These OneWorld channels will be edited in the South but aimed at a worldwide audience. The first, DebtChannel.org, focusing on Third World debt will be run from Africa. The second, LearningChannel.org, will be on education and will be produced in India.*

In 1999, to encourage net use for business and commercial reasons, China announced it was to halve charges for accessing the internet and provide a free second telephone line to all Chinese homes that already have a telephone. This was in strong contrast to the censorship employed by the Chinese government in the use of the internet. It was only in 1996 that Premier Li Peng created China's first internet law which stated that 'any direct connection with the internet must be channelled via international ports established and maintained by the Ministry of Post and Telecommunication'. Users first need to fill out a police report in triplicate. They then sign a declaration pledging not to use the internet to threaten state security or reveal state secrets, or to read or transmit material that 'endangers the state, obstructs public safety, or is obscene or pornographic'.

Infrastructure

One of the main problems to be addressed in internet connectivity in the developing world is the unreliability of electricity and telephone lines, if they exist at all. Forty-nine countries, from China to Cambodia, have less than one telephone per 100 people. In fact, there are more telephone lines in Manhattan than in the whole of sub-Saharan Africa. Problems of power surges and poor telephone connections can also hamper internet communication.

Nigeria's telephone lines, for example, can go off for days or weeks on end and rates for international telecommunication are very high. In Bosnia, on the whole, war has hindered internet development. One network that has managed to circumvent the considerable problems here is ZaMir, a network set up with the International Council of Voluntary Agencies. ZaMir has offered e-mail and conferences to predominately peace- and human rights-oriented users. Where internet infrastructure projects have been developed in the South, to provide connectivity and to promote the use of the net for women and marginalized groups within society, they have usually focused on urban areas, whilst the majority of people in, for example, Africa live in rural areas. Kampala, the capital of Uganda, has 4% of the population but 60% of the share in telephone lines.

> One of the main problems to be addressed is the unreliability of electricity and telephone lines.

Censorship

The internet can be a weapon of empowerment, bringing to ordinary people the means to find information restricted by their respective governments, the means to seek solidarity and communicate with activists in other parts of the world and the means to alert the world to abuses of human rights.

Governments fear the power of the internet, they fear that it has the capacity to precipitate the collapse of a particular regime or social order. This is taken very seriously in many repressive regimes. China, Singapore and Indonesia, for example, all operate restrictive internet policies. Singapore, whilst having a computer-skilled population, still operates a restrictive access policy under the pretext of protecting citizens from pornography. The Socialist People's Libyan Arab Jamahiriya has no internet communication and computers, telephones and fax machines all need to be registered with the government.

To see what sort of impact the net can have in the developing world and in human rights issues one only has to look at the Zapatistas example in Chapter 1. The Rand report we mentioned there notes the EZLN (Zapatista) links with NGOs:

> *The NGOs were able to form trans-border coalitions that were highly interconnected and co-ordinated to create a social netwar in the age of computers that would limit the Mexican government and would support the EZLN's cause.*

First nations of the first world?

First nations sites have flourished on the internet, providing huge amounts of information, education and activism resources and networks for first nations peoples and their supporters.

For example, Planet Peace (www.planet-peace.org) is run by indigenous community organizers and activists to distribute information regarding indigenous and environmental grass-roots initiatives from around the globe. The Indigenous Environmental Network (www.alphacds.com/ien/) is an alliance of grass-roots indigenous peoples fighting against exploitation by strengthening traditional teachings.

NativeWeb (www.nativeweb.org), one of the largest indigenous sites, has a comprehensive database of resources for and on indigenous issues, along with a community centre, native technology site and Abya Yala Net (a project of the South and Meso American Indian Rights Center). The site states:

> *NativeWeb exists to utilise the Internet to educate the public about Indigenous cultures and issues, and to promote communications between Indigenous peoples and organisations supporting their goals and efforts …
> NativeWeb is concerned with … Indigenous literature and art, legal and economic issues, land claims and new ventures in self-determination.*

Abya Yala Net (www.nativeweb.org/abyayala) is part of NativeWeb and is a network for indigenous peoples in the Americas. The site includes information and resources on indigenous peoples and their projects in Mexico, Central and South America and includes a good resource database and papers on indigenous manifestos and statements.

The People's Paths Message Center (www.yvwiiusdinvnohii.net/paths.html) hosts message boards for North American Indian communities. It also includes a web page on hoax net and urban legend stories, particularly those concerning native peoples. At the time of writing there were boards looking at various issues, including diabetes (which is believed to affect one in five native Americans), genealogy and the Cherokee nation forum which exchanges news, history, humour and educational views concerning the Cherokee community. The Syracuse board has an online forum to discuss Indian nation land issues and the Chotaw Talk board discusses education and land issues as well as providing listings on events.

The Native American Resources (www.cowboy.net/native/index.html) site provides links and information on native arts, languages, health and education issues as well as bulletin boards and mailing lists.

The Lacandon community (www.geocities.com/rainforest/3134/) of Chiapas, Mexico have created a website to present their cultural life and identity which they believe will help them be recognized as part of the worldwide struggle that faces indigenous peoples trying to save their cultures. The website is used to exchange stories and strategies with other indigenous peoples and for discussing environmental, social and political issues.

The IndigiNet Multimedia (indiginet.com.au) and InterNet Services offer a range of services designed for communities and individuals, the aim being to assist in the development of a global internet and communication system to link indigenous people at a local, national and international level in their search for self-determination.

Despite their remote geographical location the Inuit and Yupiit of the Arctic regions are networking together. The Inuit especially are very connected, using the internet not only to further political and educational debate but also to influence the future of the internet itself.

In 1998, a web-based survey was set up to learn about internet use in the Arctic regions. The survey illustrated the strengths and weaknesses inherent in usage by native peoples with little economic power and in remote geographical areas. Participants came from Arctic Alaska and Labrador, East Greenland and the Bering Strait. The average age of respondents was 34 years, with a slight bias towards male representation.

The majority lived in large settlements with access to internet providers, software and hardware and reasonably well provided telecommunication infrastructures. Small communities, while not excluded, often could not respond as their systems only supported e-mail.

The survey found that while entertainment and business scored highly in web use there was a growing number of education and networking projects going on, including online or long-distance teaching, vital health information networks and a sharing of cultures through chatrooms, bulletin boards and listservs.

The Maori, the indigenous people of Aotearoa/New Zealand, have been using the internet to help preserve their culture and language. They have set up a host of sites, from advocacy and business to news sites, digital libraries, museums, personal homepages and discussion sites on cultural property issues. For example, Muriwhenua is a well-designed site providing information on land claims in the Mud and Te Arawa areas. Small Maori community business initiatives are also using the net to market their products, such as T Pou Whakairo Enterprises which promotes performance groups, and the HEWA site for bone-carving crafts. You can also find guides to Maori genealogy and e-mail addresses of online Maori users at the Ross Himona homepage.

Preservation of language is a major concern and some sites such as the New Zealand Council for Educational Research are set up specifically to help preserve the Maori language. The site has developed a database of Maori terminology that is searchable through a web interface; in Maori the internet is called *Ipurangi*.

An issue concerning not only the Maori but many indigenous peoples is how technology, and specifically the internet, can actually cause harm to culture. Will the internet end the individual cultural values, replacing them with homogenized western consumer culture? The Indigenous Intellectual Property Constituency looks at the questions arising from the use of cultural heritage on the internet and how to protect indigenous rights within this domain.

The cultural values of indigenous peoples can come into direct conflict with western values on the net. Intellectual property rights need to take into account the concept of cultural property. At present, the digitization of cultural artefacts and images does not have to take into account the cultural owners, and the accuracy of information gathered for virtual libraries often goes on without facts being verified with the indigenous group concerned.

The Native Peoples Internet Affairs Council site represents a council made up of community leaders, elders and spokespeople for native communities in North America. Its purpose is to investigate and refute misinformation spread via the Internet on native matters and to serve as a clearing house for communication between native peoples and the mass media. The site also hosts a native e-mail contact list and details about native television and broadcasting systems.

The Maori have concerns about how many of their cultural carvings and manuscripts are being promoted on the internet and some actions on the net have resulted from this. NekeNeke e-mail list members protested by e-mail to a US tattooist who had illustrated an article on face tattoos with a selection of images of preserved Maori heads hung on meat hooks. To the Maori the human head is a sacred object and its misuse was seen as culturally offensive. The site owner was only persuaded of the offence when the author of the article, who also received notification of the e-mail campaign, protested.

Another example is when pictures of deceased Maori chiefs were placed on the net. The Maori believed that there should have been consultation with the descendants prior to this happening.

> The Maori have concerns about their cultural carvings and manuscripts being promoted on the internet.

Yet little information on the web concerning indigenous peoples comes from the people themselves, instead it is written by non-indigenous academics and educators. Indigenous communities themselves rarely have a presence on the web due to economic, literacy and geographical reasons. The Aboriginal Multi-Media Society of Alberta (AMMSA) is an independent aboriginal communications organization that aims to help facilitate the exchange of information regarding aboriginal culture including issues concerning aboriginal values, principles and traditions.

There are many sites dedicated to aboriginal issues in Australia; the majority have good links and articles ranging from land rights and history to health and deaths in custody. You can even find a site dedicated to teaching the didgeridoo at the Aboriginal Art and Cultural Centre. Through using a real audio

You can even find a site dedicated to teaching the didgeridoo at the Aboriginal Art and Cultural Centre.

player you can learn how to play this instrument. The site has been very popular with surfers all across the world.

The Council for Aboriginal Reconciliation website is used to highlight the many critical issues to do with aboriginal rights and reconciliation in Australia.

The issue of stolen children, where aboriginal children were forcibly removed from their families, is the subject of a website called The Stolen Generation (www.apology.west.net.au). The site offers an apology to Australian aborigines – over 13,400 people have used the site to send an apology by e-mail – it also offers information on reconciliation activities and events in Australia with good links to aboriginal issues and aboriginal home sites.

The Native Website is a place to bring together the tools and resources indigenous communities need in order to build communications. There is information on jobs, events, e-mail lists and chat boards.

Project Tibet is a New Mexico-based non-profit founded by Tibetan refugees in the United States. This site includes projects and stores links.

The Refworld gopher (www.unhcr.ch/refworld/welcome.htm) is the gopher service of the UNHCR's Centre for Documentation on Refugees (CDR). It includes speeches of the United Nations High Commissioner for Refugees.

Other good links

Guatemala Peace Process: www.lapaz.com.gt/
Nicaragua Solidarity Network: www.home.earthlink.net/~dbwilson/wnuhome.html
Latin America Gopher Archive: gopher://lanic.utexas.edu:70
Afghan Liberation: www.geocities.com/tokyo/ginza/3231
Sandinistas: www.sandinistas.org
FARC: www.tierra.ucsd.edu/~farc-ep/
Afro Cuba Web: http://afrocubaweb.com
Cuba Solidarity: www.igc.apc.org/cubasoli
Guerrilla Groups in Mexico: www.onr.com/user.questad/
Third World Network: www.twnside.org.sg/
Africa News: www.africanews.org
Movement for survial of the Ogoni peoples: www.oneworld.org/mosop
Southern Africa Report: www.cmpa.ca/no31.html

Burma Democracy: http://www.geocities.com/CapitolHill/4471
Free Burma Coalition: www.freeburmacoalition.org
Korea Progressive Directory: http://kpd.sing-kr.org
Alternative Information Centre (Palestine): http://aic.netgate.net
Independent Iran Observer: http://home8.inet.tele.dk/huosan/IRAN.htm
Kurdish Information Network: www.xs4all.nl/~tank/kurdish/htdocs/
Iron Wings Children – Red Holocaust: www.iwchildren.org
Links to specific tribes: http://members.tripod.com/~PHILKON/links12.html
Mohawk Nation Council: www.peacetree.com/akwesasne/home.html
NAPE Aboriginal links: Canada: www.lakeheadu.ca/~napewww/links/index.html
National Inuit Youth Council: www.maji.com/~itc/
Native Net: http://cs.fdl.cc.mn.us/natnet/
The Assembly of First Nations: www.afn.ca
Bill's Aboriginal links: www.bloorstreet.com/300block/aborl.html
Cultural Survival: www.cs.org
First Nations: People of the World: www.dickshovel.com/www.html
Fourth World Documentation Project: www.cwis.org/
Hopi Simon: www.lablinks.com/hopi/
Oneida Nation: www.oneida-nation.net/
Africa Frontline Network: www.afrikan.net

7 | Hacking, Censorship and Liberty Online

What is hacking?

In 1998 hackers in England and New Zealand protesting about nuclear tests hacked into the system at India's Bhabba Atomic Research Center. As well as downloading documents they replaced websites with a site showing a mushroom cloud and an anti-war message.

Hacking has been around as long as the internet, and while political hacking, 'hacktivism', is becoming a better-known concept it is still nascent. Many hackers now espouse political reasons but, on the whole, they are hackers first and protesters second. Hackers come in many varieties, although for most people the term 'hacker' still brings to mind the image of a hormonally-challenged adolescent plotting revenge against the world from the safety of his bedroom. A cursory reading of many of the hacker newsgroups would certainly do little to alter such a belief.

Hackers, largely, fall into three groups:

■ those who break the security of computer networks,

■ those who break the security of application software,

■ those who create malicious programs like viruses.

Primarily, in all the cases, the individuals are concerned with pitting their skills and knowledge against the programmers and software creators in companies. While reasons vary for doing so, very few see their actions as overtly political and many have gone on to, or grown up to, taking jobs with the same corporations, often advising on security measures to keep hackers at bay.

Hacking, in essence, means gaining entry to a computer system without the permission of the owner. One type of hacking includes virus building, where programs are built and used that can replicate files. For example, the very descriptive 'worms' that invade a computer and replicate themselves spreading through networks, or the Trojan horses that appear to do one thing, perhaps disguised as a handy piece of software, but that can be extremely destructive. Network hacking describes the process of infiltrating a secure site by using the site's own security measures. For example, by trying different forms of a password until the right one is accepted. Hackers can also set up 'sniffer' programs to do this; these programs are used to find encrypted information, which can then be decoded to learn more about the network.

The recent rise in hacking, especially that of Yahoo! and Ebay, has prompted US President Clinton to convene a hastily gathered internet summit where it was proposed to spend $2 billion for the 2001 fiscal year to boost cyber security, most of which would go to the Pentagon.

Certainly the US government has been subject to various types and severity of hacking with the majority of its websites being hacked at some time. For example, in June 1999 hackers defaced the US Senate website leaving the overall page integrity but changing some of the information. For example, the History Today feature was substituted for news that 'Senator Robert F. Kennedy, D-N.Y., was assassinated'.

Early in 2000 Yahoo! suffered what was described as an 'immense' network assault which brought the site down for three hours. The attack came from multiple points on the inter-

> They are hackers first and protesters second.

net, suggesting it had been co-ordinated. Other sites subject to recent cyber attacks have been Ebay, E*Trade and ZDNet, in these cases caused by a flooding of junk data which left the sites inaccessible for several hours.

The world of hacking is not mutually exclusive when it comes to sharing information and skills and some cross-over is developing between the spotty geeks and their more political savvy counterparts through bulletin boards and sites such as Cult of The Dead Cow (www.cultdeadcow.com). Dead Cow, one of the oldest hacker groups, has collaborated with political hackers on various projects. They believe that hacking can be a powerful political tool and have described hacktivism as 'a policy of hacking, phreaking or creating technology to achieve a political or social goal'. Beware, this site is believed by some to embed a virus program in your machine.

Cult of the Dead Cow is perhaps most well known for its release in 1998 of a program called Back Orifice which brought hacking to a wider audience by making it very easy to hack into Windows sys-

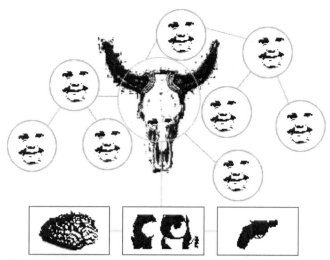

Cult of the Dead Cow

tems. Microsoft dismissed the program as being no threat to security but others in the computer industry believe differently.

At www.2600.com you will find a list of hacked websites with links to the 2600 list of hacked pages as well as sites hacked in support of East Timor and government hacked sites.

Political hacking has attracted huge amounts of publicity, but at this stage no one can be sure what the long-term effectiveness or indeed benefits may be. Hacktivism brings up many tactical and ethical questions. Commentators like Stefan Wray are at the cutting edge of critical commentary and understanding of hacktivism as both an act and a philosophy. Wray has written that hacktivism is unlikely to become an organizing tool per se, but more likely that it could be seen as a supplement to other organizing efforts by drawing attention to issues on a global scale.

There is a difference between political hacking and what is seen as electronic civil disobedience (ECD). Whilst political hackers are usually acting as individuals and under a cloak of secrecy, ECD is usually done by groups and coalitions and very openly.

Electronic civil disobedience

As discussed in Chapter 5, ECD finds its roots in the USA in the mid-1980s. The phrase comes from a group of artists called the Critical Art Ensemble, who in 1994 published their *Electronic Disturbance* essay. This and later books and articles explored the transference of physical disobedience techniques to the internet, for example, from physical sit-ins and occupations of buildings to virtual sit-ins, from pickets and protests to cyber-pickets. Instead of snail-mail letters of protest, e-mail can deliver concerns faster and perhaps more effectively as they also jam systems.

Many groups concentrate on 'denial of service' attacks. These are designed to swamp a computer network's ability to respond and perform, temporarily shutting out legitimate users. For instance, a denial of service attack on a web server floods it with bogus requests for pages and because of the demand in trying to process these requests the server is unable to respond to legitimate requests and may crash.

One proponent of electronic disobedience, which we mentioned in Chapter 5, is the Electronic Disturbance Theatre (EDT). EDT began its online life in 1988 asking supporters of the struggle for independence in Chiapas, Mexico to open the web pages of various Mexican financial companies and institutions to demonstrate international support for the Zapatistas. This was an early example of a denial of service attack or a virtual sit-in.

Since then their methods have become increasingly sophisticated and have built on a process involving a Java applet called FloodNet (see Chapter 5). They state:

The Web site of an institution or symbol of Mexican neo-liberalism is targeted on a particular day. A link to FloodNet is then posted in a public call for participation in the tactical strike. Netsurfers follow this link ... The intent is to disrupt access to the targeted Web site by flooding the host server with requests.

In September 1998, EDT launched its SWARM project. This involved a three-pronged FloodNet disturbance against websites of the Mexican presidency, the Frankfurt Stock Exchange and the Pentagon. Over 20,000 people around the globe connected to FloodNet.

Hacking for democracy

As well as the well-publicized examples of hacktivism against the Mexican government other countries have also been subject to hacking. The Indonesian government has itself been accused of waging 'cyberwar.' In January 1999, Connect-Ireland, a service provider hosting a pro-independence East Timor website, was subject to a denial of service attack and believes that sources close to the Indonesian government may have been behind the attack.

Hacking sites of totalitarian regimes has become an issue within the wider hacker community. The main topic of concern for the non-political hackers appears to surround whether political hacking breaks the 'hackers' code' or in any way helps the hacking 'cause'. At the beginning of January 1999 the International Coalition of Hackers (ICH), primarily Cult of the Dead Cow, 2006, and Chaos Computer Club, issued a joint press statement condemning the Legion of the Underground's (LOU) declaration of electronic war against the Iranian and Chinese governments. LOU first came to attention in October 1997 when it destroyed the whitepower.org (a particularly nasty white supremacist group) website.

LOU had stated in January 1999 that it was their intention to disrupt and disable the internet infrastructures of the Iranian and Chinese governments. The ICH believed this would do little to facilitate human rights and much to endanger them, especially hackers in these countries. The ICH press release read:

> *Declaring 'war' against a country is the most irresponsible thing a hacker group could do. This has nothing to do with hacktivism or hacker ethics and is nothing a hacker could be proud of.*

> *Governments worldwide are seeking to establish cyberspace as a new battleground for their artificial conflicts. The LOU has inadvertently legitimized this alarmist propaganda.*

Very soon after this statement was released LOU withdrew their campaign. It may take some lateral thinking in order to take the internal spats of hackers seriously and especially when they begin to declaim on human rights but at the same time this illustrates a shift in the paradigm for hacking and one we shall see shift considerably more in the next few years.

The great Chinese firewall

In December 1999 the founder of the China Democracy Party Wang Youcai was sentenced to 11 years' imprisonment for subversion of the state. Two of his 'crimes' were to e-mail exiled Chinese dissidents in the USA and to accept overseas funds to buy a computer.

The Great Wall of China may be more of a tourist symbol than a physical barrier to accessing China but China's electronic system of blocks and filters for the internet means the country is pretty much off limits. Earlier this year, Reuters reported that the Chinese government was stepping up its efforts to filter information available to Chinese citizens via the net. China has special internet police and distribution of pro-democracy or subversive material can mean a life sentence.

Rules have also been published which require all Chinese and foreign companies using encryption to register with the government; many believe this is the first step in a move towards a ban on all encryption technology.

China's electronic system of blocks and filters means the country is pretty much off limits.

The Chinese record in human rights and political censorship has brought about many actions of hacktivism both from Chinese dissidents and others who are prepared to do electronic battle over the control of information online. Highlighted cases such as that of Wang Youcai and Lin Hai, a software entrepreneur, have done much to bring other pro-democracy supporters into the electronic arena. Lin Hai has been branded China's first 'cyber-dissident' and charged with providing *VIP Reference* (an online parody of a Chinese Communist Party magazine) with 30,000 e-mail addresses, including those of government officials. This pro-democracy magazine is distributed throughout China by e-mail. It is sent from different addresses and distributed randomly in order to let recipients deny that they have subscribed to it. In response to his arrest, hacktivists in the USA and the UK began hacking into Chinese government websites attempting to dismantle the firewalls. Less aggressive protests have also taken place, for example in October 1999, 90,000 e-mail messages were sent to Chinese media and government officials in protest at the punishment of both Lin Hai and Wang Youcai.

War on the information highway

The work of the Rand Organization and in particular David Ronfeldt and John Arquilla demonstrates the obsession that western, if not the majority of all governments, have with the idea that the next war will be fought over and through information and by means of the internet.

Such views could be dismissed as hysteria and to date this seems to have benefited security consultants more than anyone else. But we should recognize that information is the key to power as never before. Since the development of so-called 'smart' technology and the reliance on computer-mediated technology in warfare the need to gather information electronically on the 'enemy' has become essential.

As we discussed in Chapter 1, there is a distinction between 'netwar' and 'cyberwar'. In brief, netwar refers to the war of propaganda on the internet itself. For example, this covers attempts to disrupt or damage an individual, country or group through information or misinformation and propaganda. It also encompasses in its definition the infiltration of networks and databases to promote opposition movements across computer networks.

Netwars can involve government against government or government against non-state actors and vice versa. The Zapatista movement is a good example of how successful fighting a netwar can be.

Cyberwar refers to cybernetic warfare: war dependent on computers and communications systems. In contrast to netwar, a cyberwar is primarily about conducting military operations through disrupting or destroying information systems. This is, in the lingo of the Pentagon, C4I Command, Control, Communication, Computers and Information. A good illustration of its use was during the Gulf War, when the US military used information technology to demoralize and blind the Iraqi high command.

Cyberwar is undoubtedly in capitalist terms a cheaper way of waging war. Information weapons do not rely so heavily on financial resources, information warfare has no one front line and the increasing complexity of computer networks also makes these systems more vulnerable and deterrence harder.

Privacy, censorship and freedom of expression

Privacy and censorship are enormous and complex issues and would take a book in itself to examine. At present governments and corporations are seeking greater and more rigid control of how the net is used and by whom. Not only are net-users at risk from state censorship and prying but also from information-gathering by commercial organizations. Specialist companies that trawl the net are proliferating, selling their data on you to other companies. If you buy online or if you post into a newsgroup, then unless you take steps to protect your e-mail address, these companies will create a software record of who you are. These records are then available on the net to other companies, usually for a not inconsiderable fee. For some newbie net users this has meant that no sooner have they gone online for the first time than they find their e-mail box full of 'spam' (junk e-mail), offering anything from investment opportunities to porn sites. Why? Because they have used a service that has kept a copy of their e-mail address and gone on to sell it indiscriminately.

> The Electronic Frontier Foundation is a non-profit, non-partisan organization.

The Electronic Frontier Foundation (EFF), mentioned in Chapter 1, is one of the oldest and most respected organizations working to protect online civil liberties. It is a non-profit, non-partisan organization founded in 1990 and based in San Francisco, with offices and affiliate groups across the world. Their mission is described as follows:

The Electronic Frontier Foundation has been established to help civilize the electronic frontier; to make it truly useful and beneficial not just to a technical elite, but to everyone; and to do this in a way which is in keeping with our society's highest traditions of the free and open flow of information and communication.

They continue:

The EFF also monitors legislation, provides legal advice and assistance with cases involving the defence of on-line civil liberties. It is also a charter member of the Digital Future Coalition, the Global Internet Liberty Campaign, and the Internet Free Expression Alliance.

EFF publishes an electronic bulletin, *EFFector Online*, and has a good links section on internet civil liberties and freedom of information online.

Issues of censorship have also split activists on the net, especially when it comes to hate sites. Many far-right and racist sites get hacked every month, however, some of the organizations fighting against these sites and the individuals and organizations behind them, believe it does far more damage to hack the sites than to allow the sites to exist and condemn themselves by their own words.

On 4 September 1999 the Ku Klux Klan website at www.kkk.com was replaced with the contents of the HateWatch website. HateWatch is a non-profit group campaigning against facism and racism online. HateWatch itself had nothing to do with this act especially as it believes hacking of this type is not only misguided but can damage the biggest advantage civil rights communities have on the web which is through the exposure hate groups bring to themselves.

UK threat to internet liberty

Through the Regulation of Investigatory Powers (RIP) Bill the UK government intends to make provision for the interception of communications, including making the disclosure of data such as that protected by encryption and passwords available to the security services and the police. Patricia Hewitt, the minister for e-commerce, claims these plans are 'because crime has become global and digital and we have to combat this'. However, the proposed bill will also make it a crime for individuals and organizations to take peaceful protest actions such as those mentioned in this book and the use of the internet in co-ordinating, publishing and sending out information will become, if this bill becomes law, a serious target.

Some of the most disturbing points in the proposed legislation include using Internet Service Providers (ISPs) as wire-tappers. The bill would require ISPs to disclose information on customers and to keep confidential any surveillance taking place on a customer's website or e-mail. It would be a criminal offence for an ISP to reveal to a customer that their account or website was under surveillance.

At present a wide group of UK government authorities can already collect data on you on the internet, the only exception being the actual content of your e-mail messages. The bill intends to widen these powers, and according to STAND (a coalition campaigning for safe e-commerce legislation) this will 'effectively criminalise the widespread use of encryption by making the act of losing keys or forgetting passwords a criminal offence'.

They go on to say

> *Now, let's consider this blanket permission in the light of the Internet. How much of your everyday Net communications fall into this category? Do you access your mail via Yahoo!, or Hotmail, or Netscape? Do you use ICQ, AIM or Napster? Do you subscribe to mailing lists, hosted on US machines? Do you buy shares online at Charles Schwab, or E*Trade? Do you post to USENET? ...*

If so, congratulations. The Home Secretary has just granted the security services and police permission to monitor you – with almost no legal oversight.

The STAND (www.stand.org.uk) site, set up in 1998, makes an excellent community resource for anyone interested in issues about privacy and censorship with electronic communication. The site is clear, concise and informative with a good links section for further information. It also contains an excellent list of suggestions as to what you can do to help. They have even set up a fax service to facilitate contact with your Member of Parliament, and advise on what to do if and when your MP makes contact. STAND has received a good response with over 6200 people registering to adopt their MP and putting their personalized adoption certificate on their homepage.

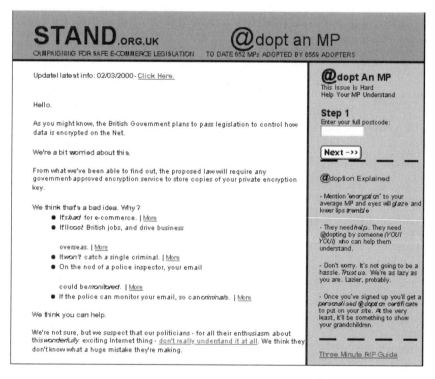

Adopt an MP

As a spokesperson for STAND says,

the MP Fax Gateway has really hit the button though, with nearly 1500 faxes sent in a month, and huge numbers of MPs requesting more information about the RIP Bill, the details of which I'll bet none of them understood at the outset.

Directly due to the site, it's safe to say that tens, if not hundreds of MPs from all sides of the house are now actively voicing concern over many measures contained in the Bill.

I think STAND.org.uk has acted more as a focal-point for individuals' existing concerns about RIP, and a conduit to let them make their views known to their elected representatives. Aside from the RIP campaign, the wider aim has always been to make it very easy for UK net users to (a) find out who their MP is and (b) contact them with near-zero expense and effort. We've never had any funding, other than donation of time, servers, bandwidth and phone bills, and we've never yet met in the same room. That said, some of the talent at our disposal was pretty outstanding (several CEOs of high-profile dot coms, well-connected net journalists, top-flight web producers and several awesome fine blaggers). There are still several core members of the campaign whom I've never met!!'

Glen Tarman of OneWorldNet shares concerns about this legislation:

The UN Universal Declaration of Human Rights, Article 19, states that 'Everyone has the right to freedom of opinion and expression; this right includes freedom to hold opinions without interference and to seek, receive and impart information and ideas through any media and regardless of frontiers.' For the first time since this 1948 proclamation of the international human right to freedom of expression, citizens of the world have the ability to exercise that right on a global basis, 'regardless of frontiers', through the internet. Governments will seek to limit the freedom of expression essential to democratic rule and civil society that have now been enhanced through new technology. Wherever authorities do try to limit the democratic potential of the internet they must be challenged particularly through international human rights law which applies to the internet just as it does to other media. Whatever issues activists campaign about online, we should always campaign on our right to do so.

An RIP Bill forum has also been set up by concerned ISPs such as GreenNet and is working with civil liberties organizations such as Liberty. As GreenNet remarks

> The RIP Bill represents a serious threat to us all. Campaigning against it will be an important part of the Association for Progressive Communications (APC) European Civil Society Internet Rights Campaign, which GreenNet is playing a major role in.

In a statement released by GreenNet in March 2000, they stated:

> The group that organised the June 18th demonstration is a GreenNet user and much of the organisation for the international protest took place using GreenNet Internet facilities. If the RIP Bill had been in place last year there seems little doubt that the police would have applied for an order to force GreenNet to give them access to the private e-mail of people involved in the June 18th events. The police would almost certainly have wanted a similar order over protest activities planned to coincide with the Seattle WTO meeting. Under the RIP Bill, they will now be able to obtain such facilities to spy on the activities of protest groups. Internet Service Providers ... will have to build 'interception capabilities' into their systems. When served with an 'interception warrant' they will be forced to intercept private e-mail and convey its contents to the police or various intelligence services.

| The RIP Bill represents a serious threat to us all. |

Project Echelon

On 21 October 1999 spy system Echelon was jammed with e-mails (see below). The actual jamming of the system was not the crucial point of the day; instead it was to alert the public to Echelon, which has been clothed in an ominous anonymity since its inception. Little is known about the use of Echelon, reports and information, mainly from whistle-blowers and leaks, are difficult to come by and very difficult to verify.

The e-mail notifying people about this event stated 'Now is a chance for anyone, regardless of computer expertise, to become an instant hacktivist – best of all, no software is needed [other than your regular e-mail program]. Here is a list of code words apparently used by "security forces" [specifically it seems the US National Security Agency who operate Menwith Hill] to sift out messages which they think they might find interesting.'

This list was extremely comprehensive so in order to prevent the reader from falling asleep we have summarized it: Waihopai, INFOSEC, ASPIC, MI6, Information Security, SAI, Information Warfare, IW, IS, Privacy, Information Terrorism, Terrorism Defensive Information, Defense Information Warfare, Offensive Information, Offensive Information Warfare, Computer Terrorism, Firewalls, Secure Internet Connections, Hackers, Encryption, Pacini, Angela, Meta-hackers, Infowar, Bubba, Freeh, Archives, Echelon, MDA, Burns, Tomlinson, Ufologico, Nazionale, nowhere.ch, Bletchley Park, Enemy of the State, SARA, Rapid Reaction, JSOFC3IP, Corporate Security, Baldwin, Electronic VIP Protection, SIG, sweep, Medco, TRD, TDR, Z, sweeping, SURSAT, Asset, Satellite imagery, force, NAIAG, Cypherpunks, NARF, 127, Coderpunks, Retinal Fetish, I R, Fetish.

Echelon is the code word given to the automated global relay and interception system used by UKUSA, an alliance of the United States' National Security Agency (NSA), the United Kingdom's Government Communications Head Quarters (GCHQ), Australia's Defense Signals Directorate (DSD), New Zealand's Government Communications Security Bureau (GCSB) and Canada's Communications Security Establishment (CSE).

> Echelon has been clothed in an ominous anonymity since its inception.

Cyber Society – http://www.unn.ac.uk/cybersociety

From: Replicant [mailto:replicant_x@yahoo.com]

Sent: Wednesday, September 29, 1999 5:09 PM

To: CyberSociety@listbot.com

Subject: HACKTIVISM: Global JAM ECHELON Day [Oct. 21]

http://www.wodip.opole.pl/~laslo/Echelon-links.html

STAND UP FOR THE FREEDOM TO EXCHANGE INFORMATION!

We the monitored have decided to stand up against the very real, very intrusive, and ultimately oppressive global surveillance system known as Echelon. Echelon is a vast mainframe set up by the New World Disorder in order to monitor the world's electronic communications for subversive keywords. Every time you send someone an e-mail with keywords like 'revolution' and 'hacktivism' [for instance], Echelon's computers make a note of it. If you forward e-mails with regularity with words on Echelon's extensive keyword list, you may be marked for human 'hands-on' monitoring.

On October 21, 1999, netizens around the globe are implored to send out at least one e-mail with at least 50 keyword words. You need not be privy to knowing exactly what words Echelon uses. It is safe to assume that words such as 'revolution' and 'manifesto' and 'revolt' [etc.] will work. Just be sure to sound as subversive as possible. There isn't even any need to write a cohesive paragraph or sentence. Echelon's computer does not understand the language anyway. It only knows to look for certain words. By doing this we can at least temporarily jam the global surveillance system'.

Echelon was a child of the cold war. Its original purpose was to protect national security, however few believe this is now its only or primary concern. In particular, it is believed that Echelon is used to prohibit and anticipate political dissent, as well as being used in industrial espionage. There is little control over Echelon outside of a few individuals in the five countries using it, a matter that not only concerns NGOs but also the European Parliament and other countries. It is allegedly capable of intercepting and processing as many as 3 billion communications every day including internet downloads, e-mails, satellite transmissions and telephone calls. Information on how Echelon works is still closely guarded, although it is believed that with the internet it employs 'sniffer' programs, devices which collect information on data packages. Outside the internet it is also reported to use massive radio transmitters to intercept satellite transmissions and satellites themselves to catch spillover data between cities. Information is then processed in the major centres in the USA (near Denver) and in the UK (Menwith Hill).

Echelon sifts all this indiscriminate information using a system called Dictionary, a computer program that finds information by searching by keyword. A European Parliament commissioned report, *An Appraisal of Technologies of Political Control*, states 'Each of the five centres supply "dictionaries" to the other four of keywords, phrases, people and places to "tag" and the "tagged" intercept is forwarded straight to the requesting country'.

A more recent report for the European Parliament, *Interception Capabilities 2000*, was prepared by Duncan Campbell in May 1999. This report makes disturbing reading for anyone with even a passing interest in protecting their civil liberties, not only online.

Further resources

'2600' is very much a central point for information on hacking and what hackers are up to. The site includes hacked websites, before and after images and links to more political hacking groups.

The Freedom of Information Act (FOIA) site in the USA has an e-mail list that was started as a service to the National Freedom of Information Coalition. To subscribe to FOI-L, send an e-mail message to: LISTSERV@listserv.syr.edu. In the body of the message, type: SUB FOI-L.

The Electronic Privacy Information Center (EPIC) works on issues to do with the protection of personal information that is electronically compiled and stored. It uses outreach by e-mail to organize coalitions and notify members when action is needed. For example it is involved in the Global Internet Liberty Campaign (GILC) which has a website at: www.gilc.org for more information on freedom of information on the net.

Usenet newsgroups

These include:

alt.activism
alt.activism.d
comp.org.eff.talk
alt.censorship
misc.activism.progressive
alt.society.civil.liberty
misc.legal
misc.legal.computing
talk.politics.crypto
alt.society.foia
alt.society.resistance
alt.freedom.of.information.act
alt.politics.datahighway.

8 Women Online

The internet raises many questions for women and women's issues. There remains a social assumption that, somehow, technology is 'masculine' and this hampers and restricts many women from going online. Poverty, race, age and disability, although factors not exclusive to women, also add to the barriers to access.

It has been argued that cyberspace is dangerous for feminism as it proliferates the patriarch and is full of pornography aimed only at men. Others argue that feminism can build on a free political space and avoid power relations. Certainly the net gives access and information to women, especially in terms of women's struggles, with sites not only devoted to women's issues (from health and reproduction to rape) but also feminist theory and critique. As well as a way to discuss and organize not only on a local but on a global scale.

While the gender gap on the internet has closed rapidly in the USA and the UK (where it is running at around 48% women at the time of writing), the gap is much larger in some countries. Sources cite figures of less than 5% in Arabic countries.

Many feminist groups have combated both the technological and financial issues themselves by setting up training and computer access points for low-income women.

> The gender gap on the internet has closed rapidly in the USA and the UK.

Fe-Mail (www.femail.org.uk) (based in Huddersfield, UK) is an initiative set up by women for women, to explore the possibilities of the internet. The site offers internet training to women who do not have computers and cannot afford the training offered by most companies. In the USA, FemiNet (www.womenspace.ca) is a women's movement network with a remit to fight women's computer illiteracy and provide training and resources to help women participate as equal online citizens. Women in Computing (WIC) (www.awc-hq.org) website gives information on what the current presence of women is in working with the internet and works towards ensuring the net is a global community not one dominated by one particular gender, race or economic/social background.

Women Leaders Online.org is an online women's activist group which aims to empower women in politics, media, society, the economy and cyberspace. The Institute for Women and Technology is also involved in attempting to increase the impact of women on technology.

Perhaps the biggest barrier, as we have said, is the underlying assumption that new technology is masculine. The culture of the net is seen as one of men: scientists, hackers, IT specialists. If the culture is seen as masculine then unfortunately this often means that education and attitudes to young girls using computers are affected too. Furthermore, men tend to dominate newsgroups and women in mixed groups often feel ignored or trivialized by men. Flaming and harassment can be part of the online experience for women, although the net also offers the anonymity and freedom they may not have experienced in real life, especially women living in rural areas or under repressive regimes.

For many women, as well as anonymity, the internet can offer time and independence. It is a less expensive way to share information and interact with other cultures and countries and to find supportive online communities. Many women's organizations first went online to cut down on costs through the use of e-mail, but now find it a good place to research and look for information on their areas of work as well as publicize and keep members informed.

Then he was a she: gender online

The question of gender on the internet is discussed endlessly both on- and off-line. The internet, many believe, can provide a genderless environment which is nothing short of empowering to women.

Yet at the same time the internet promotes a forum for global trafficking and sexual exploitation of women. Agents offer online catalogues of mail order brides; commercial prostitution tours are advertised. Pornography is widespread and perhaps the leading growth industry on the net, bringing not only still frames but live sex shows. The Coalition Against Trafficking in Women is one site concerned with these issues and attempting to fit the online into an off-line global framework. While these issues may have put many women off the internet, there is still a multitude of women's groups and views on the web. Women's groups are using internet technology for communication (within and between organizations), for lobbying, information, education and consciousness-raising.

Leading women cybernauts are keen to emphasize that the internet is not only a communication tool but a 'space' for women that can promote women's issues and equality. The majority of studies looking at reasons why women use the internet rank safety as a primary reason. For women who may feel intimidated by real-time meetings or speaking in public the net offers an anonymous and empowering way to get one's voice heard. It can create opportunities for women to explore their identity, to metaphysically 'switch' gender or to exist without gender. While there may be some truth in this, it remains foolish to think that the net is free from either racism or sexism.

But what is true is that by using the internet to create dialogue on women's issues and promote these to the world, the mainstream and often chauvinist media is omitted and uncensored information can prevail. It offers the chance for women to take control of media sources, for example Women's Wire (World-wide Information Resource and Exchange at www.womenswire.com) is a subscription-based network drawing information from the mainstream media newswires, women's organizations and government sources and giving it a women's perspective. AVIVA.org.uk is a free 'webzine' (web magazine), being run by women based in London, which provides a free listings magazine service for women as well as hosting women's groups and services.

Through the internet, feminism has a new transnational audience. For many this offers a chance to find out about a movement and history that has been censored or banned in one's home country. For example, the National Women's History Project (www.nwhp.org) is a site containing women's names and

> The net offers an anonymous and empowering way to get one's voice heard.

citing the achievements of women who were 'forgotten or were never told about'.

Thus despite the internet's reputation as a place dominated by white western men with an unhealthy interest in bizarre pornography, there is a wealth of feminist information on the web. Not only feminist discussion groups and political sites but healthcare and reproductive rights issues such as SPOT (www.critpath.org/~tracy/spot.html); the tampon health website. This site gives information on chlorine bleaching, dioxins and taxes, and offers alternatives for women that are independent of corporations and do not lead to environmental problems. The Abortion Clinics On-line (www. gynpages.com) is a US-based information site on abortion and birth control across the states. The On-line Birth Centre (www.efn.org/~djz/birth.html) offers advice and information on pregnancy, birth, midwifery and breastfeeding. It includes information for midwives, information on nutrition and pregnancy, media resources, newsgroup listings for parents and midwives and alternative health resources; it is also part of the pregnancy web-ring.

One can find vast resources and educational materials on domestic violence and violence against women, along with networks and newsgroups that support women in violent situations. VIOLET (www.violetnet.org) is a Canadian website looking at issues concerning the legal needs of abused women. The site presents legal information in various formats, from textbook style for women with an overview and understanding of the issues, to 'Mary's Story' which tells the story of an abused woman. 'It's Your Story' provides interactive software to enable the user to choose a role to learn about the law in a given situation.

There are also many feminist search engines that make looking for specific information on women's issues, advocacy and campaigning much easier. The University of Maryland Baltimore County (UMBC) Women's Studies (www.research.umbc.edu/~korenman/wmst/) website contains a huge array of resources and links and is one of the best starting points for anyone interested in women's studies. It currently has links to gender resources, activism, health, sexuality, science and technology, arts, education and social sciences among many others.

Once again the net offers unparalleled global networking. feminist.com aims to make networking via the internet easier for women by supplying listings on women's health issues, business, feminist links and reprints of congressional speeches applicable to women's issues.

The net is proving to be a wonderful place to note and publish the achievements of women through history. The feminist archives on the internet are growing and the diversity of topics is huge. The Fawcett Library (www.lgu.ac.uk/fawcett/main.htm) based in London documents the changing role of women in society and hosts reading lists and a newsletter as well as links to other women's sites across the world. The Bristol-based Feminist archive (www.femarch.mcmail.com) includes photographs, drawings, postcards, calendars and personal letters of feminist material from the 1960s to today.

There are many political resources for women on the net, and of these anarchist feminism resources are the biggest, with information ranging from the anarchist theory on women's oppression, to Spanish women anarchists and the works of Emma Goldman. For example, the Mujeres Libres list (meaning 'free women' in Spanish) is a listserv for anarchist women to meet in cyberspace, to exchange information and learn about each other's struggles.

> Feminist action sites are all over the internet.

Feminist action sites are all over the internet ranging in themes from environmental politics to gender, from sexuality issues to cyberpolitics. Virtual Sisterhood (www.igc.apc.org/vsister) provides a web space to enable the creation of a global networking of women for women's activism, including issues concerning inclusion and empowerment of women and development of women's online resources.

Cyberfeminism

VNS Matrix's Cyberfeminist Manifesto for the 21st Century states: 'we are the virus of the new world disorder/rupturing the symbolic from within/saboteurs of big daddy mainframe/the clitoris is a direct line to the matrix...'.

One of the biggest movements currently online concerns cyberfeminism and through this the claiming of technology for women. A good place to start is at the Old Boys Network site (www.obn.org). It gives a good idea as to what cyberfemism is about. Many in the cyberfeminist movement have alienated traditional feminist support by their repudiation of, and in some cases scorn for, the feminist movements of the 1970s.

The question of how to define cyberfeminism has brought about many contradictory positions within both feminist policy and women working in computers. In plain language, it would seem that cyberfeminism could be described as a movement that focuses on the material, political, emotional and sexual conditions arising from women's place within society and that this must be linked with the means to take control of one's destiny via the internet.

The First Cyberfeminist International took place in Kassel, Germany on 20–28 September 1997. A statement released at the Kassel conference said 'The First Cyberfeminist International slips through the traps of definition with different attitudes towards art, culture, theory, politics, communication and technology – the terrain of the Internet'.

Some good resource sites

www.smartgirl.com is a good site for young women who want to find out what is on the internet.

gurl at www.gurl.com is a great site for teenage girls with good, informative and interestingly written articles on body image and teenage issues.

The Old Boys Network mentioned above describes itself as the first international cyberfeminist organization, 'a virtual and real coalition of Cyberfeminists'. Their website is incredibly well designed and has a good FAQ sheet on what they see as cyberfeminism.

femina.cybergrrl.com has been described as a Yahoo! for women, and indeed it has an incredible listing section on everything from politics to literature and the arts.

The Assault Prevention Information Network (www.yehundit/org/apinintro.html) is a good US site for information on sexual assault and abuse.

Lesbian.org has many links to lesbian organizations.

Jewish Feminist Resources (www.world.std.com/~alevin/ jewishfeminist.html) has links to organizations, periodicals and information.

The Feminist Majority Foundation's (feminist.org) *Newsbytes* has abbreviated daily news from multiple sources.

Sojourner (www.Sojournal.org) provides 'feature articles, interviews, viewpoints, reviews, fiction and poetry by and of interest to women' on their website.

B.a.B.e., Be Active Be Emancipated (www.interlog.com/moyra): this is the website of a group working for women's human rights and especially the legal status of women in Croatia.

The Native American Women's Health Education Resource Centre works on education and health.

The Black Women in Sisterhood for Action (BISA) (www.feminist.com/bisas.html) work for educational and career development for black women.

WomensNet (www.igc.org/igc/gateway/wnindex.html) is part of the IGC network and provides a global community space for women and women's issues, along with a calendar of events and campaigns and headline news on women's issues throughout the world. Their links section is very comprehensive and a good place to look for feminist activist resources.

Sistahspace (www.sistahspace.com) is a site created to try and dispel stereotypes concerning black women and to assist and encourage black women to access the internet and create their own homepages.

HerSPHERE (members.aol.com/afriwoman/hersphere) is a resource site for black women and looks at relevant issues in the visual arts, literature, business, politics and technology.

Third-World-Women Web-ring (www.pitt.edu/~gajjala/twww.html) works to connect third-world women's sites and through this to create a more visible presence on the internet. The sites are primarily concerned with economic and cultural issues for women.

The feminism bulletin board system '**The Room of One's Own**' (www.islandnet.com/room/enter) was established on 1 December 1995 in Taiwan. The site aims to provide space for female net users to discuss women's issues. In addition to examining internet issues, the site also has a searchable gopher on gender subjects as well as providing information on women's history, child-rearing and work.

> WomensNet provides a global community space for women and women's issues.

The Ethnic Woman International (www.thefuturesite. com/ethnic/index) is an online magazine that documents the struggles of women internationally against poverty and sexism.

The Women's International Electronic University (www.wvu.edu/~womensu/) is a site intended to empower women by increasing access to online education. The site acts as a clearing house to locate courses for students.

Rural Womyn (www.wowwomen.com/ruralzone/frontpage.html) is an online community of rural feminists with information on sustainable agriculture, global gender and rural issues.

Women- and Gender-Related Electronic Forums (www-unix.umbc.edu/~korenman/wmst/forums.html) is a great resource for finding mailing lists relating to women's issues and is well worth a look before joining e-mail forums.

At **Feminist Activist Resources on the Net** (www.igc.apc.org/women/feminist.html) you will find resources on reproductive rights, politics, health and global issues.

The Global Fund for Women (www.globalfundforwomen.org) is an international organization which focuses on female human rights. Their mission is to: listen to the concerns of women's groups globally; provide women's groups with financial and other resources; increase support for women's efforts globally; develop and strengthen links among women's groups worldwide; heighten awareness of the needs and strengths of women.

Discussion lists

Women's newslists abound; often they are seen as safer places to discuss feminist issues than newsgroups, as it is more difficult for them to be spammed or receive hate mail. There have been so many instances of men seeking access to female-only discussion groups that some of them now issue an online test to try and find out if a prospective member is really a man. Perhaps, still the best newsgroup for feminists is soc.feminism, a moderated pro-feminist newsgroup which has been in existence for many years. Alt. feminism is dominated by people who are against feminism and as an unmoderated group is not for the sensitive.

Perhaps the best newsgroup for feminists is soc.feminism.

The Marxism-feminism list was created by the Spoon collective (http://lists.village.virginia.edu/~spoons/) to provide a forum for discussion of feminist socialists, and issues concerning feminist relationships with Marxism. The list informs us that typical examples of some of the topics intended for discussion include:

- the relationship of Marxist-feminist politics in and outside of the academy, especially issues concerning the so-called division between 'theory' and 'practice';

- the necessity of establishing a feminist methodology that does not isolate or privilege gender at the expense of class and race, instead of the usual ineffectual 'listing' of differences in place of serious discussion of the ways that they inform our very notion of 'gender' as such;

- a (re)evaluation of Marx's and Engels' positions on gender and the family, especially in relation to Marxist and non-Marxist feminists' treatment of these issues;

- the present position of women in the international marketplace, especially the role of gender in the international division of labour; what new modes of gender/class exploitation have arisen as a consequence of the intensive global expansion of capitalism in all its new and increasingly destructive forms.

FEMAIL (femail-request@lucerne.eng.sun.com), a moderated list, 'exists to provide a shared communication channel for feminists around the world'.

FEMINISM-DIGEST makes the Usenet newsgroup soc.feminism available in digest form via e-mail for those who either cannot access Usenet or prefer the digest format. To subscribe to the digest, send a request to Feminism-digest@ncar.ucar.edu (Internet).

Unruly Women (www.topica.com/lists/unrulywomen/) is a women-only mailing list for women who have personal and bad experiences of the mental health system.

SOUTH ASIAN WOMEN'S NET (Susnac@hel/2.NIH.ga) is a female-only discussion group for women from the south Asian countries as well as women from other parts of the world interested in the concerns of south Asian women.

SAPPHO (Sappho-request@mc.lcs.m17.edu) is a forum and support group for gay and bisexual women. Membership is open to all women and is limited to women.

9 | Alternative Media

Publishing costs money. For small independent magazines and newspapers publishing is very much an ongoing struggle. In the UK, it is very difficult to reach a broad audience because distribution is expensive and, in many cases, the larger news- and bookstores simply will not take small independent publications. For magazines and journals that eschew mainstream advertising and want to maintain integrity the print media world is often fraught with difficulties.

Yet, in order for activism, both on and off the net, to succeed there need to be ways of getting information out to individuals and other groups. The web and e-mail are now playing a significant role in facilitating this.

When it comes to informing the general public, the old media outlets are used by the majority of NGOs and activists. However, the propaganda and agenda of many media outlets has meant information given to the media has been twisted and misinterpreted and many activists have become wary and mistrusting of the press.

For example, the media attention garnered by the 18 June Carnival against Capitalism was for the most part in the UK very distorted. Further, some newspapers have formed an unholy alliance with the many internet security consultants who make it their interest to hype up how the internet is being used by activists to bring down social order through violent means.

While it is true that the net creates many opportunities for hurting a company where it really matters (financially), physical violence is rarely on the agenda.

The majority of groups campaigning and protesting, both on and off the web, are committed to non-violent practices, so it is little wonder that they are disillusioned with the mainstream media. It is also a fact that it has only been since late 1999 that activists have begun to really harness the power of the internet for action and protest.

As OneWorldNet comments

The mainstream media has tended to report the use of the Internet in a sinister way. It's a classic panic over a new media. What they tend to ignore is that most legitimate protests are based around very open communications and often public meetings where anyone can attend. Seattle was a watershed because it made visible the global movement for change and that individuals and organizations were connecting with each other across the world. Now the internet is where democratic alternatives that put people and the planet before profit are being discussed and planned.

The mainstream media has tended to report the use of the internet in a sinister way.

There is a growing realization that if you want a story published then you do it yourself or use alternative channels to do so. Take for example David Shayler, an ex-MI5 agent, now living in self-imposed exile in France. At the time of writing Shayler cannot return to the UK; if he does, he faces imprisonment for breaching the Official Secrets Act. His 'crime' was to reveal the truth behind many MI5 activities and the undemocratic nature of the organization. Accepting that it is breach of the Official Secrets Act and other injunctions in the UK, by finding a European web server he has been able to publish his allegations on his site www.shayler.com, alerting not only UK citizens but also people across the world.

The breadth and quality of alternative news on the web is amazing, from single-issue e-zines to e-mail lists on genetics, poverty and corporate practices, and downloadable newsletters on the environment. The internet provides a cheap way of circumventing the mainstream press and their interests to produce news which is accessible and without censorship.

Red Pepper (www.redpepper.org.uk), with which one of the authors of this book is associated, is predominantly a print mag-

> **If you want a story published then you do it yourself.**

azine. However, with increasing difficulties in circulation we have begun to develop our website as not only an adjacent and added extra to the magazine or indeed, a way of generating interest in the print magazine but as a 'product' in its own right. This means we are creating a site that not only provides information and links but is also interactive with debate and involvement for readers. Some ways in which we are doing this include bulletin boards and chatrooms on topics concerning UK and international politics, green issues and community action. Other sites have progressed even further and in this chapter we will look at a few examples that not only illustrate the vibrancy and potential for news through the internet but show that even with little money, but with some imagination, there are huge possibilities for the smallest of groups.

Recently Red Pepper has set up a debate for readers through OneList. OneList provides a list forum for groups and individuals. By logging into OneList you can create your own group to discuss any topic under the sun, your forum can be moderated or unmoderated, open to the public or have closed access to just the people you invite. It takes a lot of the pain out of using your own

Red Pepper

listserv and for smaller groups for reasons of time and resources it makes sense to use a forum like OneList. Our debate focused on the mayoral elections in London on 4 May 2000. It is a way to garner opinions and discuss options and repercussions; not only is it good to encourage debate but it helps the magazine by bringing in fresh opinions and perspectives.

Resources

For UK activists a site that really should be visited regularly is that of Squall, which has maintained a web presence since 1995. Squall (www.squall.co.uk) started as a print newsletter offering independent and trustworthy news to activists and campaigners on UK law, politics and human rights. However, due to difficulties in distribution and prohibitive costs, they took the decision to move onto the web. Jim Carey of Squall believes the internet provides them not only with an answer to distribution and costs but also extends their reach globally. He goes further, believing that the net is unique; whereas newspaper copy would end up the next day as a wrapper for fish and chips (unhygienic as this may sound to non-British readers), the internet gives longevity to stories, building a huge encyclopaedia of knowledge, open to anyone with a modem. He sees the internet as still embryonic, especially in the UK where connectivity is far from free, and believes even though web-media has exploded in recent years the future is still open as to where this will lead. In making the decision to go online, Squall had to accept that perhaps as many as 85% of their existing readers might disappear simply because they had no access, but they believed that not only would they gain a huge new audience but as time progressed these readers would return. Squall has created an incredibly impressive site; as Jim says 'If you want to find out about direct action in the UK over the last ten years you would either go to Squall for more in-depth commentary or SchNews for shorter articles'. Jim believes that right now, and most definitely in the future, trustworthy, factual and reputable news sources such as Squall can stand against the might of CNN and Fox, simply because of the quality and reputability of the material. For anyone new to the internet finding their feet among the vast body of information, sites like Squall stand out. They believe they have found their niche. As Jim Carey says, only slightly glibly, journalism creates the first draft of history. Squall wants to ensure this means the real story.

SchNews is another trusted and active alternative media source in the UK. In November 1999 SchNews got hold of the Bilderberg papers, concerning the secret group of world leaders. The papers outline their plans for the future of the world as they see it. As SchNews says 'just sit back and let the words speak for themselves'. The site lets you download the complete version. SchNews also publishes a very informative newsletter on the web and a printed version for off-line distribution along with some excellent guides on activism.

Another great UK activist sites and source for activist news is Urban 75 (www.urban75.com), a brilliant UK magazine of direct action. It offers practical advice and information on activism from road construction and genetically modified food to action against multinationals and underground news from activists.

As we have mentioned, the effectiveness of the alternative media could really be seen at the Seattle protests on 30 November 1999. Indiemedia, a coalition including the Direct Action Media Network (DAMN), harnessed 400 writers and journalists to take to the streets of Seattle directly reporting on actions taking place. The footage recorded is now available on CD-ROM.

Certainly censorship is a huge issue in terms of alternative media and news. At present the internet allows this freedom but as the STAND site points out, at least in the UK, for how long? The proposed RIP bill discussed in Chapter 7 has received very little mainstream news coverage, yet in the UK it represents a huge threat to uncensored and free information.

> Censorship is a huge issue in terms of alternative media and news.

In the USA one of the biggest sites on the net for alternative media and resources is ZNet. Started by Michael Albert of *Z Magazine* the site hosts a monthly magazine with a forum where Noam Chomsky and other radicals discuss events in the news. The site is the online project of *Z Magazine* and says without boasting that 'ZNet presents analyses, but also vision. It provides diagnosis but also prescription'. At the time of writing there are about 1000 articles, various discussions and chat, reviews of books and films, good and in-depth resource sections on race, ecology, gender and class plus alternative media coverage and even a song lyrics facility.

Another good site to check out is the A-Infos site which offers a collection of mailing lists and web pages for anarchists and the news they might find of interest.

CounterMedia is a US site bringing information on protests and actions that you will not find in the traditional media. As they say on their site 'We'll document community struggles and protests as they occur, help reporters find out about demonstrations and local organizing campaigns, and make video images, photographs and reports available to mainstream media outlets and the alternative press, both locally and nationally'. Members of the coalition behind it include Active Resistance, Earth First and Freespeech TV.

The World Wide Free Press offers an online reader-written publication. It reports on and encourages activities designed to increase social, cultural, economic and political rights. 'It is an independent voice, a mirror of truth, helping all organizations promoting social change to grow by providing their friends and critics with a public forum for discussion and planning and evaluation.'

Other resources

Left Business Observer is a monthly newsletter giving information on the political economy. It is available on the net or through a print subscription.

Digital Freedom Network publishes banned, censored and sensitive political documents from all over the world.

Fairness and Accuracy in Reporting is an organization providing objective news and information not covered by the print and television media.

The Tactical Media Crew (www.tmcrew.org) is a collective of media and political activists based in Rome. Although major parts of the site are in Italian they do have some English language pages. They believe the media must be addressed in a very tactical way, covering stories on technology, Echelon and the CIA among others. There is also material on McDonald's, Shell, Nestlé and Glaxo and links to Italian social centres.

The Direct Action Media Network is a multimedia news service covering direct actions. DAMN attempts to place its coverage within both a historical and contemporary context.

The Project-Censored-L listserv is a moderated list that will send information about censored stories in the USA and general censorship issues.

The Alternative Press Centre is a non-profit collective providing access and increasing public awareness of the alternative press.

Using the media: some helpful hints

E-mail press releases

Before using e-mails for press releases remember that press relations need to be built over a period of time and like everyone else the press do not like to be spammed.

If you have had no previous relationship with a publication always send a short e-mail letting an editor know that a release is ready and can be viewed on your website and offer to send them a copy.

If you are sending an unsolicited e-mail do not send attachments – especially big ones. We know from being on the receiving end. During press week a big attachment can really slow up our ability to get in copy, or even worse crash our system. Unsolicited attachments will not endear you to publishers. Instead provide a URL where the information can be viewed.

Print publications will more often than not have some kind of forward planning or editorial calendar. See if you can request a copy to see what sort of features are planned for the year. That way you can schedule topical releases.

Remember, like any form of press release yours needs to grab attention; be short and to the point. This is particularly important with e-mail, as scanning a long e-mail message can often be difficult in a time-pressured environment. Ten lines or fewer are preferable. Try to use short paragraphs, as, again, it is easier on the eye with an e-mail.

Another bugbear is formatting. Many people overwrap lines. Make the message as simple as possible, left-justified with line breaks at 65 characters.

Finally, relevance, back to spamming. Never just send a press release out to every journalist that you know; make sure the material is relevant otherwise the next time you do have something relevant to say it may simply be zapped without being read. There is nothing wrong with sending a preliminary e-mail first asking what a particular magazine or newspaper's procedure is, in fact it is a good way to start building a relationship. And whatever you do, and however tempting, try not to send repeated e-mails asking 'Did you get my e-mail?'.

We'll continue our discussion of using e-mail for activism in the following chapter.

> If you are sending an unsolicited e-mail do not send attachments.

Part Two

Building Your Web: How to Get Online and Use the Internet

10 Using E-mail for Activism

E-mail is a powerful tool for activists because it is cheap, effective and accessible. There are three main ways in which e-mail can benefit an activist organization:

- generic use, to improve efficiency;
- one-way e-mail lists, to quickly and cheaply 'broadcast' information;
- two-way e-mail lists, to promote discussion and planning.

Generic use: improving efficiency

E-mail is fast (messages are received within seconds, minutes or hours), cheap (you can communicate a lot of information for less than the price of a stamp), easy and environmentally friendly (by reducing paper usage). E-mails are less disruptive than telephone calls and easier to reply to than letters. For these reasons, switching as much letter and telephone communication as possible to e-mail will pay tremendous dividends in the amount you can achieve with limited time and money at your disposal.

One of the most potent uses of the net for a small organization is to use e-mail for fund-raising applications. Most grant-giving organizations will e-mail you the materials, and then accept your application via e-mail. The time savings will let you make more applications in the same time.

One-way e-mail lists

> E-mail is the perfect vehicle for one-to-many communication.

E-mail is the perfect vehicle for one-to-many communication, like sending out an action alert or a newsletter, as you can send the same thing to hundreds or even thousands of people for the same cost as sending it to just one person.

Some organizations have taken the view that they shouldn't use e-mail until all of their supporters are online, as it creates a two-tier system of communication. While this can be a legitimate concern, it is worth thinking about the benefits. For example, if you send out a monthly newsletter to 1000 people, and each newsletter costs 50p in paper, envelope, copying and postage, that costs you £6000 a year. If 30% of the recipients are online, and you use e-mail for those 30%, you'll save £1800 per year.

We describe below some of the most effective ways in which you can use one-way e-mail lists.

E-mail newsletters

Newsletters not only keep members and volunteers informed, but if you fund-raise are a good way of keeping your donors up to date on what your group is doing. At a sophisticated level, you can have more than one newsletter dependent on purpose and who it is going to be sent to.

Surveys

Use e-mail to find out what your membership wants and thinks about issues, or for internal planning and organization.

Event notification

Create a regular announcement list which lets people know what's going on. Send the same information to lots of people much more quickly than telephoning around.

Media contact

Using e-mail to contact the media can be very effective. E-mail is an easy and cost-effective way to send press releases, whether to e-papers or the printed paper.

Build website traffic

Send out regular bulletins by e-mail when you update your site, letting people know that there is a new page or new information available on the site.

Action alerts

An action alert is a message calling for specific action to be taken. E-mail action alerts are modelled on telephone trees but are much cheaper and quicker to use. They have the added benefit in that recipients can forward on the alert to other people who they think will be able to do something.

> An action alert is a message calling for specific action to be taken.

While e-mail action alerts are a phenomenally powerful tool for activists, and have been used to great effect by organizations like Amnesty International, considerable care needs to be taken in their use. The following guidelines may be helpful:

1. Include clear information about yourself and prove your authenticity by providing ways to be traced such as an e-mail address, URL, postal address or telephone number.

2. Put a date on your message. As an e-mail can travel around the internet for a very long time sometimes you can get a situation where the alert is many months old but is still being forwarded on by concerned people as there is no date on the original. Remember headers tend to get changed and deleted when forwarded.

3. Include clear beginning and ending markers. Text can be paraphrased when it is sent on, often changing the message entirely; this can easily discredit your original alert.

4. Make sure all the information is in the text. You may know the issue so well that you forget that other people will not. Set up a web page if you can that gives more information and clearly signpost this. Tell the whole story and try to link it to wider issues of social justice in order

to show how it relates to different causes. Even if a person doesn't act on the message they will know more about the issue this way and may act in the future.

5. Make sure you ask for something feasible and well defined. For example, if you ask people to contact an MP, then give the name and address of this person or details of where to find this out if their local representatives live in different areas of the country to where the alert is focused.

6. Don't create panic or rant. If the alert is time-critical then say this, but don't use capital letters and emotive wording.

7. Avoid sounding hectoring or self-righteous, especially if e-mailing other activists who may feel you are preaching to the converted.

8. Make your message easy to read. Use a simple, clear layout with lots of white space. Break up long paragraphs. If you send out regular alerts try and get a format that makes your message and group distinctive.

9. Lead readers to further information; give website addresses of where they can find more information on the subject, or address and telephone numbers of campaign groups who can help.

10. Include a phrase like 'post where appropriate' and emphasize that people should not post to lists that have no relevancy.

11. If your information is sensitive and you don't want the alert forwarded to other lists, make sure you say so.

12. Ask people to get back to you with any action they have taken; ask them to send back copies of any letters they write or e-mails they send, or response they get from meetings and telephone conversations. You need to evaluate your strategy and monitor alerts to see if they work and how they could be improved.

13. Never send unsolicited mass e-mailings and never post action alerts to e-mail discussion lists or Usenet groups on unrelated issues.

14. Do not just rely on the internet. Remember it is only one tool, not the only one.

15. Always include detailed information on how subscribers can unsubscribe, and who to contact if there are problems.

Peace Brigades International emergency response network has an e-mail list component allowing urgent action requests to be sent out across the world rapidly and cheaply. Action alerts and electronic newsletters can be forwarded to relevant discussion lists and newsgroups. For an example, see http://dlis.gseis.ucla.edu/people/pagre/alerts.html.

Two-way e-mail lists

E-mail lists can also be two-way, so that any replies sent to the list are forwarded to everyone who received the original, thus creating many-to-many communication. This can be extremely effective not only in enabling decisions to be made by groups of people scattered around the country, but also in promoting a sense of belonging among a broader membership.

> E-mail lists can also be two-way.

The three main uses of two-way lists are described below.

Closed lists of small groups

Committee members are often spread across a town or city, making physical meetings relatively infrequent. If everyone is on e-mail, much of the discussion and decision-making can be done via e-mail, not only maintaining momentum between meetings but also reserving the meetings for the issues which require greatest discussion.

Coalition groups

Coalition groups rarely have the time or the money to meet often, making e-mail an excellent way to keep informed and share information and strategy.

Large, open e-mail lists

One of the most powerful ways of using an e-mail list is to create a forum which any supporter can join. By encouraging discussion and planning, list members often take a much more active role in the organization.

If you opt for an open list, a few guidelines may again be helpful:

1. Stay focused. Ensure your list is focused on the topic at hand. It is very easy to go off topic and if your list is too broad many messages will fall outside the main subject of interest. This then causes people to get annoyed, stop reading and end up by not responding to anything. If an issue is likely to become a burning topic of interest only to a minority, create a separate list.

2. Encourage people to keep messages short. Again it is easy to generate lots of messages.

3. Never subscribe people to your list without first asking their permission.

A word about online petitions

Petitions are a contentious subject in cyberspace. A major problem concerns their origins; often they are sent out by people with little scope for verification and sometimes the facts are wrong or scaremongering. Petitions are also difficult to co-ordinate as they go in different directions and the originator will need to sort through thousands of names, often on multiple copies. Think long and hard before using a petition, it may seem like a good idea at the time but often they generate more ill-will then good. If you must do it, make sure your petition has an expiry date so it is not travelling the world ad infinitum.

> Petitions are a contentious subject in cyberspace.

How to create an e-mail list

The simplest way to create an e-mail list is to use your e-mail software's address book to create an e-mail address with multiple recipients.

For a one-way list, put your own address in the 'To' field and then everyone else's address in the 'Bcc' (blind carbon copy) field. This will ensure that people cannot see the names of the other recipients. Include a note which asks people not to do a 'Reply-to-all'.

For a two-way list, ask people to use their e-mail software's Reply-to-all function to send the reply to everyone on the list.

However, CC-lists (carbon copy) have many limitations. One of the most important of these is that you have to do all the work in terms of adding and removing people to and from the list, updating e-mail addresses and so on. For a large list, this can generate a lot of work.

Second, people make mistakes. They use Reply-to-all on one-way lists, and forget to do so on two-way lists.

Third, for two-way lists, all the e-mail goes via you. So your e-mail load goes up significantly, and people only receive replies when you go online.

For these reasons, it is usually better to use what is known as a listserv or list server. A listserv automates most of the administration, and means that people get replies straightaway. In the days of old, running a listserv required both a permanent net connection and a bit of technical wizardry. These days, anyone can create a list using one of the commercial websites designed for this purpose. If you're willing to put up with banner ads on the website used to configure the list, and small text ads in your e-mails, these are a real boon.

The biggest of the free commercial listservs is OneList (www.onelist.com). It takes about 15 minutes to register, create and configure a list. Once it's done, you just give people the web address OneList will supply. You can, however, choose to control who joins the list, and can even set things so that you have to approve all postings if you want to.

You also get free shared filespace, a calendar of events, message archives and even a chatroom. All the instructions can be found on the website. An alternative to OneList is ListBot (www.listbot.com).

You can also join public lists. You'll find about half a million of these at OneList alone!

Newsgroups

Newsgroups are another form of public list. Some e-mail software allows you to use newsgroups, otherwise you can do so from the E-mail/News part of your web browser.

There are many tens of thousands of newsgroups worldwide, covering almost every subject imaginable.

You can search for internet discussion groups relating to your organization and mission at www.liszt.com or at www.dejanews.com.

Participating in public lists and newsgroups

Most public lists and newsgroups have a set of rules which participants are expected to respect, so it is worth taking the time to familiarize yourself with them.

With lists, you'll normally be e-mailed a copy of the rules when you join. With newsgroups, it's worth 'lurking' (reading without contributing) for a week or two so that you get a feel for the group and see the rules posted.

With both lists and newsgroups, there are some generally-accepted unwritten rules known as 'netiquette'. The most important of these are:

- Post only in plain text. You may need to check your software to make sure that it is sending plain text, not HTML. *Never* send attachments to a public list or newsgroup – these can take a long time to download and are a major nuisance.

- Be polite. If you wish to disagree with someone, do so via reasoned argument, not personal attack.

- Quote intelligently. When replying, it's useful to leave in the relevant bits of the original message, but cut the rest of the message to prevent everyone else receiving it twice.

- Respect confidentiality. Don't post a message you received via e-mail to a public list or newsgroup without permission.

- Stay on topic. Don't post action alerts on vivisection to a list or newsgroup about political prisoners.

- Don't forward unverified messages. There are a great many hoax messages floating around the internet. Some of them have been going for many years. In particular, don't forward a virus alert unless you are qualified to verify the source: almost all of these are hoaxes.

Intranets and electronic networks

Intranets and electronic networks are common in workplaces. They enable a specific group of computer users to communicate online, but they are not part of the larger internet. Non-profit organizations and grass-roots groups can also set up these types of networks. A couple of examples worth visiting are: PeaceNet at **www.peacenet.org/** and HandsNet at **www.handsnet.org/**.

Spam – unsolicited e-mail

No one appreciates junk e-mail and your e-mails may be seen as junk if sent to the wrong group. It is also easy for a new group to become an e-mail spammer by default and you can risk alienating the very people you are trying to reach by putting people on your list without their consent.

> No one appreciates junk e-mail.

Recommended actions

1. Solicit e-mail addresses from members, volunteers, the press and individuals and groups you meet at meetings, conferences and actions. Establish a database of contacts just as you would with postal addresses and telephone numbers. Do this by:

   (a) adding a space for e-mail addresses to membership forms, leaflet and information request forms;

   (b) making sure everyone in your group is briefed about securing e-mail addresses from people they are in contact with;

   (c) publicizing your e-mail address so people know they can respond to you by e-mail.

2. Establish e-mail lists. Use more than one list. The types of lists, as discussed in our e-mail list section above, could include one or more of the following:

   (a) general list for information about your issues;

   (b) updates list on actions, meetings and seminars;

   (c) action alerts list for activists;

   (d) newsletter list for members;

   (e) interactive discussion, to allow communication between different members of your organization.

3. It is best to start with no more than two lists – one for members and one for activists. Both can be broadcast lists – this means one-way communication as opposed to interactive discussion. As you get used to using lists add a general list for information with an automatic responder so anyone inquiring about what you do can get it. Such a list requires little updating and management.

4. Establish an interactive discussion list to facilitate communication with members, activists and volunteers or staff. This list will need much more input and you will need to make sure someone takes responsibility for its management but it is ideal to discuss feedback on action alerts, strategies for campaigns and proposals for further actions.

5. Create a website that initially focuses on providing information for your existing membership and activists.

6. Integrate the website with your e-mail lists. In your action alerts and broadcast lists make sure you make reference to your website and post documents of relevancy to the alert on the site. If you are working with other groups who have websites then give the URLs of these groups. Post your action alerts on your website as well as notifying through your list.

11 How to Create a Website

After e-mail, the web is the second most powerful tool for activists. A website can enable you to get your message across to tens of thousands of people at virtually no cost to you!

The CD accompanying this book contains a 'website kit'. This chapter explains how to use the kit to create a basic website within a few hours, and has some guidance on developing your site over time.

There are only four steps to using the supplied kit to create your website:

1. Take a look at the demo site on the CD.

2. Edit the text of the demo pages.

3. Upload the files to your internet account.

4. Publicize your site.

Take a look at the demo site

Open the folder called **Website Kit** and double-click on the file called **index.html**. This will launch your web browser and show you the first page of the website, the Welcome page:

The first thing you will notice is that the web page is divided in two with a black menu-bar at the top and the main page below.

In the menu-bar, the only thing you need to change is the name of your organization. In the main page, you don't have to change anything at all unless you want to, but you can change the text if you wish and – if you have a scanner – you can scan in your logo to replace the globe. We explain how to do both below, but first let's look at the rest of the site. Click on **About us** and you'll get this page:

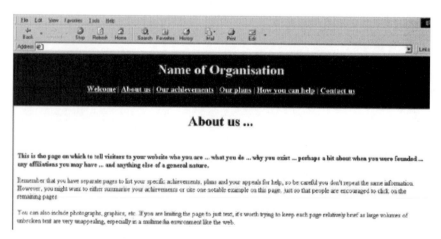

If you now click on **Our achievements** you get this:

And so on for the rest of the site. Take a look at the remaining pages now to familiarize yourself with the purpose of each page.

Edit the text of the web pages

To turn the demo site into a website for your organization, all you have to do is to copy the files to your hard drive and edit the text in each of the HTML files. You don't need to understand HTML to do this as we've provided some software to do it for you.

First of all, open the CD and copy the folder called **Website Kit** onto your hard drive (double-click on the CD to open it, single-click on the **Website Kit** folder and drag it onto your C: drive).

Now, on the CD, double-click on **Microsoft Frontpage Express**. You will see a screen like this:

You don't need to understand HTML.

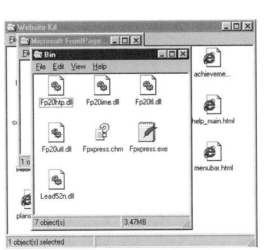

Click the yellow folder icon (or go to the **File** menu and select **Open**) and you'll see a dialogue like this:

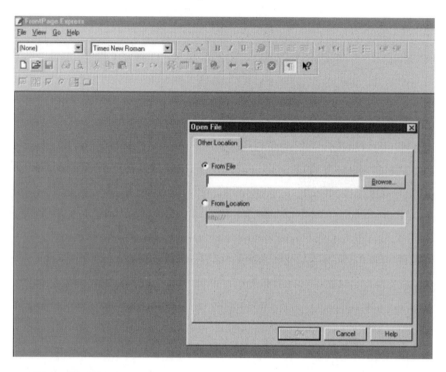

Click the **Browse** button and navigate to your C: drive, open the **Website Kit** folder and then click on the file called **menubar.html**:

Click the Open button and you will see this:

You can now highlight **Name of Organisation**, delete it and replace it with the name of your organization. When you have

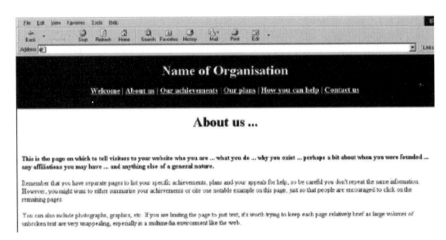

done this, click the floppy disk icon (or go to the **File** menu and click **Save**). This change will now affect every page (the same menu-bar is included on every page of your website).

Next, edit the About page of your website. Do this by clicking the yellow folder icon (or going to the **File** menu and selecting **Open**), clicking the **Browse** button again and this time high-lighting the file called **about_main.html** (*not* the file called 'about.html'). You will now see this:

Edit the About

page of your

website.

You can edit this text in the usual way, using the guidelines shown there to help you compose your own text.

Repeat this for each of the following files:

- **achievement_main.html**
- **plans_main.html**
- **help_main.html**
- **contact_main.html.**

If you want to edit the text on the Welcome page, then do the same for **index_main.html.**

If you have a scanner and want to put your logo on the web-site, scan your logo as a JPEG and call the scanned image **logo.jpg**. Make the image reasonably small, and stick to a reso-lution of about 72 dpi – anything more than this and the web page will be slow to load. Once you have the **logo.jpg** file, put it in the **Website Kit** folder (say **Yes** when asked if you want to overwrite the existing file).

You now have a website on your hard drive. To test it, double-click on the file **index.html** and that will open the website in your browser and you'll be able to navigate through it exactly as other people will when it is on the internet.

Upload the files to your internet account

All you have to do to make your website live is to upload the files to your internet homepages space. Your ISP will need to explain how to do this as the process varies slightly from provider to provider, but it isn't difficult.

Once you have the instructions from your ISP, just upload all of the files in the **Website Kit** folder (but not the folder itself). As soon as you have done this, your website is live on the internet!

Publicize your site

> You need to let the world know that [your website] is there.

A website makes information about you accessible to millions of people on the internet, but it doesn't mean that those millions are actually visiting your site. You need to let the world know that it is there.

Members and people who already know you

■ Add your URL to all your stationery: business cards, letterheads, leaflets, media releases, fax cover sheets and so on.

■ When you send e-mails make sure you have your website address at the bottom.

■ Send out the information in a newsletter or mailing to your membership.

■ Identify like-minded websites and e-mail the webmaster your URL, asking whether they would be willing to provide a link to your site.

People who do not know you

When you go to a search engine and enter keywords, your website will not be found. This is because the search engines don't yet know that your site exists. If you do nothing, they will eventually find it, but it is much quicker if you tell them about it by registering your site.

To register your website, go to each of the main search engines and look for their 'Register' facility. The main search engines to visit are:

- Alta Vista (www.altavista.com)
- Excite (www.excite.com)
- Hotbot (www.hotbot.com)
- Infoseek (www.infoseek.com)
- Yahoo! (www.yahoo.com).

You can also get yourself added to dozens of other search engines in one go by registering your site at: www.submit-it.com.

Send out a media release to the local or national press letting them know about your web site and what information it contains; ask local papers to put a small piece about this in their paper.

What next?

Although the website kit we provided will give you a basic web presence, you will probably want to expand the site over time. Other pages you might want to add include:

- action alerts
- links to other sites
- current newsletter
- archives of past newsletters
- media releases
- personal stories and photographs
- FAQs section
- simple graphics to make your site visually appealing (but keep the files small!).

> The search engines don't yet know that your site exists.

> There are
> numerous sites
> on the web that
> can be of help.

To expand your site beyond the pages supplied on the CD, you'll have to learn a bit about web-authoring. There are numerous books and resources dedicated to this. The newsgroup comp. infosystems.www.authoring.html is a good place to ask for recommendations and advice.

There are also numerous sites on the web that can be of help. Some of these are:

- AlertBox column on website usability (www.useit.com/alertbox/)

- Apple Web Design Guidelines (applenet.apple.com/hi/web/web.html)

- Yale Web Style Guide (info.med.yale.edu/caim/manual/contents.html)

- Web Developers' Virtual Library (www.stars.com/)

- HTML Goodies (http://htmlgoodies.com/).

Domain names

If using your particular Internet Service Provider means that your URL is something like www.ispname.com/users/homepages/ yourname/, then you may want to get your own domain name. There are lots of companies that can do this for you – just do a search under 'domain names' to find companies in your country. You could then have a URL like www.yourname.org.

Try to think of a short and simple version of your organization's name. You should tell the domain name company that you want a '.org' address so that visitors know that you are a nonprofit organization.

Other quick-and-easy tips

Finally, there are a few things you can do to further publicize your site:

- Participate regularly in relevant e-mail lists and newsgroups to offer relevant answers to queries. Make sure your signature carries details of your website and e-mail addresses.

- If your ISP provides website logs, monitor the number and type of people visiting your site. This can help you see how successful your marketing efforts are, and where adjustments need to be made.

- Invite visitors to leave you their e-mail address and ask for permission to send updates.

- Ask visitors to bookmark your site and to pass on the URL to others who may be interested.

Monitor the number and type of people visiting your site.

Index